Algebra 1

**LARSON
BOSWELL
KANOLD
STIFF**

Applications • Equations • Graphs

*Practice Workbook
with Examples*

The Practice Workbook provides additional
practice with worked-out examples for every lesson.
The workbook covers essential skills and vocabulary.
Space is provided for students to show their work.

McDougal Littell
A HOUGHTON MIFFLIN COMPANY
Evanston, Illinois • Boston • Dallas

ISBN: 0-618-02063-2

16 - VEI - 08 07 06

Contents

NAME _____ DATE _____

Practice with Examples

For use with pages 3–8

GOAL Evaluate a variable expression and write a variable expression that models a real-life situation

---

VOCABULARY

A **variable** is a letter that is used to represent one or more numbers.

The numbers are the **values** of the variable.

A **variable expression** is a collection of numbers, variables, and operations.

Replacing each variable in an expression by a number is called **evaluating the expression.**

Writing the units of each variable in a real-life problem is called **unit analysis.**

EXAMPLE 1 *Evaluating a Variable Expression*

Evaluate the expression when $y = 3$.

a. $y - 5$ **b.** $12y$

SOLUTION

a. $y - 5 = 3 - 5$ Substitute 3 for y.   **b.** $12y = 12(3)$ Substitute 3 for y.

　　　　$= -2$ Simplify.　　　　　　　　　　　　$= 36$ Simplify.

Exercises for Example 1

Evaluate the expression for the given value of the variable.

1. $8 + x$ when $x = 6$ **2.** $\dfrac{10}{s}$ when $s = 2$ **3.** $0.2a$ when $a = 20$

4. $9 - y$ when $y = 1$ **5.** $\frac{3}{4}q$ when $q = 12$ **6.** $8b$ when $b = 3$

Chapter 1

Practice with Examples

For use with pages 3–8

Chapter 1

EXAMPLE 2 *Evaluating a Real-Life Expression*

You deposit $300 in a bank account that pays an annual interest rate of 2.5%. How much simple interest will you earn after two years?

SOLUTION

Simple interest $= Prt$	Write expression.
$\qquad = (300)(0.025)(2)$	Substitute 300 for P, 0.025 for r, and 2 for t.
$\qquad = 15$	Simplify.

After two years, you will have $15 of simple interest.

Exercises for Example 2

7. You deposit $250 in a bank account that pays an annual interest rate of 2%. How much simple interest will you earn after two years?

8. You deposit $140 in a bank account that pays an annual interest rate of 3.5%. How much simple interest will you earn after one year?

Algebra 1
Practice Workbook with Examples

NAME _____ DATE _____

Practice with Examples

For use with pages 3–8

EXAMPLE 3   *Modeling a Real-Life Situation*

If you are driving at a constant speed of 65 miles per hour, how long will
it take you to travel 325 miles?

SOLUTION

Verbal Model
$$\text{Time} = \frac{\text{Distance}}{\text{Rate}}$$

Labels
Time = t (hours)
Distance = 325   (miles)
Rate = 65   (miles per hour)

Algebraic Model
$$t = \frac{325}{65} \qquad \text{Write algebraic model.}$$
$$= 5 \qquad \text{Simplify.}$$

It should take you 5 hours to travel 325 miles.

Exercises for Example 3

9. If you are driving at a constant speed of 60 miles per hour, how long will it
   take you to travel 270 miles?

10. Find the average speed for an airplane traveling 2100 miles in 6 hours.

Chapter 1

NAME _____ DATE _____

Practice with Examples

For use with pages 9–14

GOAL Evaluate expressions containing exponents and use exponents in real-life problems

---

VOCABULARY

An **expression** like 2^3 is called a **power,** where the **exponent** 3 represents the number of times the **base** 2 is used as a factor.

Grouping symbols, such as parentheses or brackets, indicate the order in which operations should be performed.

EXAMPLE 1 *Evaluating Powers*

Evaluate the expression y^4 when $y = 3$.

SOLUTION

$y^4 = 3^4$ Substitute 3 for y.

   $= 3 \cdot 3 \cdot 3 \cdot 3$ Write factors.

   $= 81$ Multiply.

The value of the expression is 81.

Exercises for Example 1

Evaluate the expression for the given value of the variable.

1. q^3 when $q = 10$ **2.** b^5 when $b = 2$ **3.** z^2 when $z = 5$

4. x^4 when $x = 6$ **5.** m^3 when $m = 9$ **6.** n^5 when $n = 3$

Algebra 1
Practice Workbook with Examples

NAME _____ DATE _____

Practice with Examples

For use with pages 9–14

EXAMPLE 2 *Exponents and Grouping Symbols*

Evaluate the expression when $x = 2$.

a. $3x^4$

b. $(3x)^4$

SOLUTION

a. $3x^4 = 3(2^4)$ Substitute 2 for x.

      $= 3(16)$ Evaluate power.

      $= 48$ Multiply.

b. $(3x)^4 = (3 \cdot 2)^4$ Substitute 2 for x.

      $= 6^4$ Multiply within parentheses.

      $= 1296$ Evaluate power.

Exercises for Example 2

Evaluate the expression for the given values of the variables.

  7. $(c + d)^3$ when $c = 2$ and $d = 5$

  8. $c^3 + d^3$ when $c = 2$ and $d = 5$

  9. $5p^2$ when $p = 2$

  10. $(5p)^2$ when $p = 2$

Chapter 1

Practice with Examples

For use with pages 9–14

EXAMPLE 3 *Finding Volume*

A storage crate has the shape of a cube. Each edge of the crate is 1.5 feet long. Find the volume of the crate in cubic feet.

SOLUTION

$V = s^3$ Write formula for volume.

   $= 1.5^3$ Substitute 1.5 for s.

   $= 3.375$ Evaluate power.

The volume of the storage cube is 3.375 ft^3.

Exercises for Example 3

11. The formula for the area of a square is $A = s^2$. Find the area of a square when $s = 10$ ft.

12. The formula for the volume of a cube is $V = s^3$. Find the volume of a cube when $s = 6$ in.

13. The formula for the area of a square is $A = s^2$. Find the area of a square when $s = 5.2$ cm.

14. The formula for the volume of a cube is $V = s^3$. Find the volume of a cube when $s = 3.5$ ft.

Algebra 1
Practice Workbook with Examples

NAME _____ DATE _____

Practice with Examples

For use with pages 16–22

 GOAL Use the order of operations to evaluate algebraic expressions and use a calculator to evaluate real-life expressions

VOCABULARY

An established **order of operations** is used to evaluate an expression involving more than one operation.

EXAMPLE 1 *Evaluating Expressions Without Grouping Symbols*

    a. Evaluate $5x^2 - 6$ when $x = 3$.

    b. Evaluate $7 + 15 \div 3 - 4$.

SOLUTION

    a. $5x^2 - 6 = 5 \cdot 3^2 - 6$ Substitute 3 for x.

                $= 5 \cdot 9 - 6$ Evaluate power.

                $= 45 - 6$ Evaluate product.

                $= 39$ Evaluate difference.

    b. $7 + 15 \div 3 - 4 = 7 + (15 \div 3) - 4$ Divide first.

                       $= 7 + 5 - 4$ Evaluate quotient.

                       $= 12 - 4$ Work from left to right.

                       $= 8$ Evaluate difference.

Exercises for Example 1

Evaluate the expression.

1. $4 \cdot 3 + 8 \div 2$

2. $24 \div 6 \cdot 2$

3. $21 - 5 \cdot 2$

NAME _____ DATE _____

Practice with Examples

For use with pages 16–22

EXAMPLE 2 *Evaluating Expressions With Grouping Symbols*

Evaluate $24 \div (6 \cdot 2)$.

SOLUTION

$$24 \div (6 \cdot 2) = 24 \div 12 \qquad \text{Simplify } 6 \cdot 2.$$
$$= 2 \qquad \qquad \text{Evaluate the quotient.}$$

Exercises for Example 2

Evaluate the expression.

4. $(6 - 2)^2 - 1$

5. $30 \div (1 + 4) + 2$

6. $(8 + 4) \div (1 + 2) + 1$

7. $6 - (2^2 - 1)$

8. $(30 \div 1) + (4 + 2)$

9. $8 + 4 \div (1 + 2 + 1)$

Algebra 1
Practice Workbook with Examples

LESSON

1.3
CONTINUED

NAME _____ DATE _____

Practice with Examples

For use with pages 16–22

EXAMPLE 3 *Calculating Family Admission Prices*

Use the table below which shows admission prices for a theme park.
Suppose a family of 2 adults and 3 children go to the park. The children's
ages are 6 years, 8 years, and 13 years.

a. Write an expression that represents the admission price for the family.

b. Use a calculator to evaluate the expression.

Theme Park Admission Prices	
Age	*Admission price*
Adults	$34.00
Children (3–9 years)	$21.00
Children (2 years and under)	Free

SOLUTION

a. The admission price for the child who is 13 years old is $34, the adult price.
The family must buy 3 adult tickets and 2 children's tickets. An expression
that represents the admission price for the family is $3(34) + 2(21)$.

b. If your calculator uses the established order of operations, the following
keystroke sequence gives the result 144.

$3 \boxed{\times} 34 \boxed{+} 2 \boxed{\times} 21 \boxed{\text{ENTER}}$

The admission price for the family is $144.

Exercise for Example 3

10. Rework Example 3 for a family of 2 adults and 4 children. The children's
ages are 2 years, 4 years, 10 years, and 12 years.

Chapter 1

NAME _____ DATE _____

Practice with Examples

For use with pages 24–30

 GOAL **Check solutions of equations and inequalities and solve equations using mental math**

VOCABULARY

An **equation** is formed when an equal sign is placed between two equal expressions.

An **open sentence** is an equation that contains one or more variables.

When the variable in a single-variable equation is replaced by a number and the resulting statement is true, the number is a **solution of the equation.**

Finding all the solutions of an equation is called **solving the equation.**

An **inequality** is formed when an inequality symbol is placed between two expressions.

A **solution of an inequality** is a number that produces a true statement when it is substituted for the variable in the inequality.

EXAMPLE 1 *Checking Possible Solutions of an Equation*

Check whether the numbers 2 and 4 are solutions of the equation $2x + 3 = 11$.

SOLUTION

To check the possible solutions, substitute them into the equation. If both sides of the equation have the same value, then the number is a solution.

x	$2x + 3 = 11$	Result	Conclusion
2	$2(2) + 3 \stackrel{?}{=} 11$	$7 \neq 11$	2 is not a solution
4	$2(4) + 3 \stackrel{?}{=} 11$	$11 = 11$	4 is a solution

The number 4 is a solution of $2x + 3 = 11$. The number 2 is not a solution.

Exercises for Example 1

Check whether the given number is a solution of the equation.

1. $5p - 2 = 12$; 3

2. $8 + 2y = 10$; 3

3. $3a + 2 = 14$; 2

4. $\dfrac{t}{4} - 3 = 0$; 12

5. $n + 4n = 20$; 5

6. $k + 7 = 3k + 1$; 3

Algebra 1
Practice Workbook with Examples

NAME _____ DATE _____

Practice with Examples

For use with pages 24–30

Chapter 1

EXAMPLE 2 *Checking Solutions of Inequalities*

Decide whether 6 is a solution of the inequality.

a. $3 + w \geq 9$ **b.** $r + 4 > 11$

SOLUTION

Inequality	Substitution	Result	Conclusion
a. $3 + w \geq 9$	$3 + 6 \overset{?}{\geq} 9$	$9 \geq 9$	6 is a solution
b. $r + 4 > 11$	$6 + 4 \overset{?}{>} 11$	$10 \not> 11$	6 is not a solution

Exercises for Example 2

Check whether the given number is a solution of the inequality.

7. $2f - 3 \geq 8; \ 5$

8. $2h - 4 > 10; \ 3$

9. $13x \leq 6x + 15; \ 2$

NAME _____ DATE _____

Practice with Examples

For use with pages 24–30

EXAMPLE 3 *Using Mental Math to Solve an Equation*

Which mental math question could be used to find the solution of the equation $x - 7 = 15$?

A. What number can be subtracted from 7 to get 15?

B. What number can 7 be subtracted from to get 15?

C. What number can 15 be subtracted from to get 7?

SOLUTION

Because 7 can be subtracted from 22 to get 15, mental math question B could be used to solve the equation $x - 7 = 15$.

Exercises for Example 3

Write a question that could be used to solve the equation. Then use mental math to solve the equation.

10. $z + 7 = 21$ **11.** $3f + 1 = 19$

12. $a - 12 = 10$ **13.** $\dfrac{y}{3} = 11$

14. $4j - 7 = 9$ **15.** $\dfrac{b}{2} = 4$

NAME _____ DATE _____

Practice with Examples

For use with pages 32–39

 GOAL Translate verbal phrases into algebraic expressions and use a verbal model to solve a real-life problem

> **VOCABULARY**
>
> Writing algebraic expressions, equations, or inequalities that represent real-life situations is called **modeling**. The expression, equation, or inequality is a **mathematical model** of the real-life situation.

EXAMPLE 1 *Translating Verbal Phrases into Algebra*

Translate the phrase into an algebraic expression.

SOLUTION

a. Four more than half of a number n

$4 + \frac{1}{2}n$ Think: 4 more than what?

b. Twelve decreased by a number y

$12 - y$ Think: 12 decreased by what?

c. The quotient of eight and a number w

$\dfrac{8}{w}$ Think: The quotient of 8 and what?

Exercises for Example 1

Write the verbal phrase as an algebraic expression. Use x for the variable in your expression.

1. Eight less than half of a number

2. A number decreased by five

3. Product of ten and a number

4. Seven squared increased by a number

5. Quotient of a number and sixteen

6. Difference of a number and two

Chapter 1

NAME _____ DATE _____

Practice with Examples

For use with pages 32–39

Writing an Algebraic Model

Movie theater tickets cost $6 each. One day, the total receipts from ticket sales were $420. How many tickets were sold?

Write an equation to model the situation. Use mental math to solve the equation for the number of tickets sold.

SOLUTION

Verbal Model

| Cost per ticket | · | Number of tickets | = | Total receipts |

Labels   Cost per ticket = 6   (dollars)

Number of tickets = n (tickets)

Total receipts = 420   (dollars)

Algebraic Model $6n = 420$

$n = 70$

The number of tickets sold was 70.

Chapter 1

Practice with Examples

For use with pages 32–39

Exercises for Example 2

In Exercises 7 and 8, do the following.

a. **Write a verbal model.**
b. **Assign labels and write an algebraic model based on your verbal model.**
c. **Use mental math to solve the equation.**

7. The student government is selling baseball hats at $8 each. The group wants to raise $2480. How many hats does the group need to sell?

8. You and your two sisters bought a gift for your brother. You paid $7.50 for your share (one-third of the gift). What was the total cost of the gift?

NAME _____ DATE _____

Practice with Examples

For use with pages 40–45

GOAL **Use tables to organize data and use graphs to organize real-life data**

Chapter 1

> ### VOCABULARY
>
> The word **data** is plural and it means information, facts, or numbers that describe something.
>
> **Bar graphs** and **line graphs** are used to organize data.

EXAMPLE 1 ***Using a Table to Organize Data***

The data in the table show the number of passenger cars produced by three automobile manufacturers.

Passenger Car Production (in thousands)						
Year	**1970**	**1975**	**1980**	**1985**	**1990**	**1995**
Company A	1273	903	639	1266	727	577
Company B	2017	1808	1307	1636	1377	1396
Company C	2979	3679	4065	4887	2755	2515

a. During which 5-year period did the total passenger car production decrease the most?

b. During which 5-year period did the total passenger car production increase the most?

SOLUTION

Add two more rows to the table. Enter the total passenger car production of all three companies and the amount of change from one 5-year period to the next.

Year	1970	1975	1980	1985	1990	1995
Total	6269	6390	6011	7789	4859	4488
Change		121	−379	1778	−2930	−371

a. From the table, you can see that the total passenger car production decreased the most from 1985 to 1990.

b. From the table, you can see that the total passenger car production increased the most from 1980 to 1985.

NAME _____ DATE _____

Practice with Examples

For use with pages 40–45

Exercises for Example 1

1. Use the data from Example 1. During which 5-year period did the total passenger car production decrease the least?

2. Use the data from Example 1. During which 5-year period did the total passenger car production increase the least?

EXAMPLE 2 *Using Graphs to Organize Real-Life Data*

Use the data from Example 1. Draw a line graph to organize the data for Company A's passenger car production.

a. During which 5-year period did Company A's passenger car production decrease the least?

b. During which 5-year period did Company A's passenger car production decrease the most?

SOLUTION

Draw the vertical scale from 0 to 1400 thousand cars in increments of 200 thousand cars. Mark the number of years on the horizontal axis starting with 1970. For each number of passenger cars produced, draw a point on the graph. Then draw a line from each point to the next point.

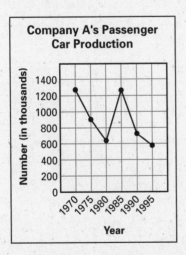

a. Company A's passenger car production decreased the least from 1990–1995.

b. Company A's passenger car production decreased the most from 1985–1990.

Chapter 1

NAME _____ DATE _____

Practice with Examples

For use with pages 40–45

Exercises for Example 2

In Exercises 3 and 4, use the data from Example 1.

3. Draw a line graph to organize the data for Company C's passenger car production. During which 5-year period did Company C's passenger car production decrease the most?

4. Draw a line graph to organize the data for Company B's passenger car production. During which 5-year period did Company B's passenger car production increase the most?

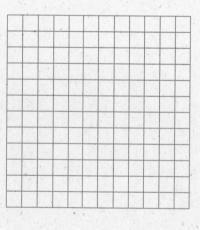

NAME _____ DATE _____

Practice with Examples

For use with pages 46–52

Identify a function, make an input-output table for a function, and write an equation for a real-life function

---

VOCABULARY

A **function** is a rule that establishes a relationship between two quantities, called the **input** and the **output**. For each input, there is exactly one output.

Making an **input-output table** is one way to describe a function.

The collection of all input values is the **domain** of the function.

The collection of all output values is the **range** of the function.

EXAMPLE 1 *Identifying a Function*

Does the table represent a function? Explain.

Input	Output
5	1
5	2
10	3
15	4

SOLUTION

The table does not represent a function. For the input value 5, there are two output values, not one.

Exercises for Example 1

In Exercises 1 and 2, does the table represent a function? Explain.

1.

Input	Output
1	4
2	8
3	12
4	16

2.

Input	Output
1	5
2	6
2	7
3	8

NAME _____ DATE _____

Practice with Examples

For use with pages 46–52

EXAMPLE 2 *Making an Input-Output Table*

Make an input-output table for the function $y = 3x + 1.5$. Use 0, 1, 2, and 3 as the domain.

SOLUTION

List an output for each of the inputs.

INPUT	FUNCTION	OUTPUT
$x = 0$.	$y = 3(0) + 1.5$	$y = 1.5$
$x = 1$	$y = 3(1) + 1.5$	$y = 4.5$
$x = 2$	$y = 3(2) + 1.5$	$y = 7.5$
$x = 3$	$y = 3(3) + 1.5$	$y = 10.5$

Make an input-output table.

Input x	Output y
0	1.5
1	4.5
2	7.5
3	10.5

Exercises for Example 2

In Exercises 3–5, make an input-output table for the function. Use 0, 1, 2, and 3 as the domain.

3. $y = 5 - x$

4. $y = 4x - 1$

5. $y = 2 - x$

Algebra 1
Practice Workbook with Examples

NAME _____ DATE _____

Practice with Examples

For use with pages 46–52

Chapter 1

EXAMPLE 3 *Writing an Equation*

The county fair charges $4 per vehicle and $1.50 for each person in the vehicle. Represent the total charge C as a function of the number of persons p. Write an equation for the function.

SOLUTION

Verbal Model

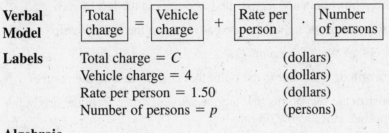

$$\boxed{\text{Total charge}} = \boxed{\text{Vehicle charge}} + \boxed{\text{Rate per person}} \cdot \boxed{\text{Number of persons}}$$

Labels
Total charge $= C$ (dollars)
Vehicle charge $= 4$ (dollars)
Rate per person $= 1.50$ (dollars)
Number of persons $= p$ (persons)

Algebraic Model $C = 4 + 1.5p$

Exercises for Example 3

6. Rework Example 3 if the vehicle charge is $1.50 and $4 is charged for each person in the vehicle.

7. Rework Example 3 if the vehicle charge is $3 and $2.50 is charged for each person in the vehicle.

Practice with Examples

For use with pages 63–70

GOAL **Graph and compare real numbers using a number line and find the opposite and the absolute value of a number in real-life applications**

VOCABULARY

Real numbers can be pictured as points on a horizontal line called a **real number line.**

Negative numbers are represented as points to the left of zero.

Positive numbers are represented as points to the right of zero.

Integers are any of the numbers . . . $-3, -2, -1, 0, 1, 2, 3$ . . .

The **graph** of a number is the point that corresponds to the number.

Opposites are two points that are the same distance from the origin but on opposite sides of the origin.

The **absolute value** of a real number is the distance between the origin and the point representing the real number.

Velocity, which indicates both speed and direction, can be positive or negative.

EXAMPLE 1 *Graphing and Comparing Real Numbers*

Graph -3 and 2 on a number line. Then write two inequalities that compare the two numbers.

SOLUTION

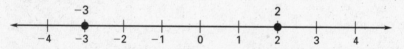

On the graph, -3 is to the left of 2, so -3 is less than 2.

$$-3 < 2$$

On the graph, 2 is to the right of -3, so 2 is greater than -3.

$$2 > -3$$

Exercises for Example 1

Graph the numbers on a number line. Then write two inequalities that compare the two numbers.

1. -4 and -7 **2.** -2.3 and -2.8 **3.** 5 and -6

Practice with Examples

For use with pages 63–70

EXAMPLE 2 · *Ordering Real Numbers*

Write the following numbers in increasing order: 3.5, −3, 0, −1.5, −0.2, 2.

SOLUTION

First graph the numbers on a number line.

```
        −3      −1.5  −0.2 0              2        3.5
    ┼────●───┼────●───┼─●●─┼────┼────●────┼────●────┼──▶
   −4      −3      −2      −1    0    1    2    3    4
```

From the graph, you can see that the order is −3, −1.5, −0.2, 0, 2, 3.5.

Exercises for Example 2

Write the numbers in increasing order.

4. $2, -3, -2.5, 4.5, -1.5$

5. $-\frac{3}{4}, \frac{1}{4}, -2, -\frac{5}{4}, 1$

EXAMPLE 3 · *Finding the Opposite and the Absolute Value of a Number*

a. Find the opposite of each number: 3.6 and −7.

b. Find the absolute value of each number: 3.6 and −7.

SOLUTION

a. The opposite of 3.6 is −3.6 because each is 3.6 units from the origin. The opposite of −7 is 7 because each is 7 units from the origin.

b. The absolute value of 3.6 is 3.6. The absolute value of −7 is 7 because the absolute value of a number represents distance, which is never negative.

Exercises for Example 3

Find the opposite of the number. Then find the absolute value of the number.

6. -1.7

7. 4.2

8. -5

Algebra 1
Practice Workbook with Examples

23

Chapter 2

Practice with Examples

For use with pages 63–70

EXAMPLE 4 *Finding Velocity and Speed*

An elevator descends at a rate of 900 feet per minute. Find the velocity and the speed of the elevator.

SOLUTION

Velocity = -900 ft per min   Motion is downward.

Speed = $|-900| = 900$ ft per min   Speed is positive.

Exercises for Example 4

Find the speed and the velocity of the object.

9. A duck hawk descends at 150 miles per hour when striking its prey.

10. A balloon descends at 17 feet per second when landing.

Chapter 2

NAME _____ DATE _____

Practice with Examples

For use with pages 72–77

GOAL Add real numbers using a number line or rules of addition and solve real-life problems using addition

EXAMPLE 1 ## *Adding Real Numbers*

Use a number line to find the sum: $4 + 1 + (-3)$.

SOLUTION

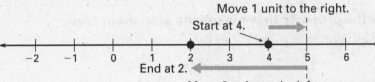

The sum can be written as $4 + 1 + (-3) = 2$.

Exercises for Example 1

Use a number line to find the sum.

1. $-8 + 6$ **2.** $-5 + (-1)$ **3.** $10 + (-4)$

4. $9 + (-3) + (-2)$ **5.** $-2 + (-4) + (-1)$ **6.** $6 + 1 + (-7)$

Chapter 2

Algebra 1
Practice Workbook with Examples

Practice with Examples

For use with pages 72–77

EXAMPLE 2 **Using Rules and Properties of Addition to Find a Sum**

Find the sum: $3.8 + (-1.2) + 1.2$.

SOLUTION

$3.8 + (-1.2) + 1.2 = 3.8 + (-1.2 + 1.2)$ Use associative property.

$= 3.8 + 0 = 3.8$ Use identity property and property of 0.

Exercises for Example 2

Name the property that makes the statement true.

7. $(-6) + (-7) = (-7) + (-6)$

8. $5 + 0 = 5$

9. $(-4 + 8) + 6 = -4 + (8 + 6)$

10. $13 + (-13) = 0$

NAME _____ DATE _____

Practice with Examples

For use with pages 72–77

EXAMPLE 3 *Using Addition in Real Life*

The temperature rose 5°F from 7 A.M. to 11 A.M., rose 2°F from 11 A.M. to 5 P.M., then fell 6°F from 5 P.M. to 10 P.M.

Use the properties of addition and the rules of addition to find the overall change in temperature.

SOLUTION

The overall change in temperature is represented as $5 + 2 + (-6)$.

$$
\begin{aligned}
5 + 2 + (-6) &= (5 + 2) + (-6) && \text{Use associative property.} \\
&= 7 + (-6) && \text{Simplify.} \\
&= 1 && \text{Add two numbers with opposite signs.}
\end{aligned}
$$

The overall change in temperature, a rise, can be written as 1°F.

Exercises for Example 3

11. A bookstore had a first-quarter profit of $342.60, a second-quarter loss of $78.35, a third-quarter loss of $127.40, and a fourth-quarter profit of $457.80. Did the store make a profit during the year? Explain.

12. The price of a share of stock increased $3.00 on Monday, decreased $1.25 on Wednesday, and decreased $2.00 on Friday. Find the overall change in the price of a share of the stock.

Chapter 2

NAME _____ DATE _____

Practice with Examples

For use with pages 79–85

GOAL Subtract real numbers using the subtraction rule and use subtraction of real numbers to solve real-life problems

---

VOCABULARY

The **terms** of an expression are the parts that are added when the expression is written as a sum.

EXAMPLE 1 *Using the Subtraction Rule*

Find the difference.

a. $-2 - 6$ **b.** $-1 - (-9)$

SOLUTION

a. $-2 - 6 = -2 + (-6)$ Add the opposite of 6.

            $= -8$ Use rules of addition.

b. $-1 - (-9) = -1 + 9$ Add the opposite of -9.

            $= 8$ Use rules of addition.

Exercises for Example 1

Find the difference.

1. $2 - 5$ **2.** $-5 - 7$

3. $2.5 - 4$ **4.** $4 - 2.5$

5. $10 - 2$ **6.** $10 - (-2)$

Chapter 2

NAME _____ DATE _____

Practice with Examples

For use with pages 79–85

EXAMPLE 2 *Evaluating Expressions and Finding the Terms of an Expression*

   a. Evaluate the expression $-8 - 3 - (-10) + 2$.

   b. Find the terms of the expression $-8 - 3x$.

SOLUTION

   a. $-8 - 3 - (-10) + 2 = -8 + (-3) + 10 + 2$ Add the opposites of 3 and -10.

                     $= -11 + 10 + 2$ Add -8 and -3.

                     $= -1 + 2$ Add -11 and 10.

                     $= 1$ Add -1 and 2.

   b. $-8 - 3x = -8 + (-3x)$ Rewrite the difference as a sum.

When an expression is written as a sum, the parts that are added are the terms of the expression. The terms of the expression are -8 and $-3x$.

Exercises for Example 2

Evaluate the expression.

   7. $5 + (-3) - 1$ **8.** $9 - (-2) + 7$ **9.** $-6 - 2 + (-5)$

Find the terms of the expression.

   10. $7 - 4x$ **11.** $-y - 5$ **12.** $-2a + 1$

Chapter 2

Practice with Examples

For use with pages 79–85

EXAMPLE 3 *Using Subtraction in Real Life*

You record the daily high temperature for one week. The temperatures (in degrees Fahrenheit) are given in the table. Find the change in the temperature from each day to the next to complete the table.

Day	Sun	Mon	Tue	Wed	Thu	Fri	Sat
High Temperature	72	75	70	67	71	72	68
Change	—	?	?	?	?	?	?

SOLUTION

Subtract each day's temperature from the temperature for the previous day.

DAY	HIGH TEMPERATURE	CHANGE
Sun	72	—
Mon	75	$75 - 72 = 3$
Tue	70	$70 - 75 = -5$
Wed	67	$67 - 70 = -3$
Thu	71	$71 - 67 = 4$
Fri	72	$72 - 71 = 1$
Sat	68	$68 - 72 = -4$

Exercise for Example 3

13. The amount of snowfall is recorded for each week in the month of January. The amounts (in inches) are given in the table. Find the change in the amount of snowfall from each week to the next to complete the table.

Week	1	2	3	4
Amount	9	6.5	11	14
Change	—	?	?	?

Algebra 1
Practice Workbook with Examples

NAME _____ DATE _____

Practice with Examples

For use with pages 86–91

GOAL Organize data in a matrix and add and subtract two matrices

---

VOCABULARY

A **matrix** is a rectangular arrangement of numbers into horizontal rows and vertical columns.

Each number in a matrix is called an **entry.**

EXAMPLE 1 *Writing a Matrix*

Write a matrix to organize the following information about your collection of books.

Hardback	5 mysteries	10 science fiction	2 history
Paperback	8 mysteries	13 science fiction	7 history

SOLUTION

Hardback and *Paperback* can be labels for the rows or for the columns.

As Row Labels:

$$\begin{array}{c} & \text{Mysteries} & \begin{array}{c}\text{Science}\\\text{Fiction}\end{array} & \text{History} \\ \text{Hardback} & \begin{bmatrix} 5 & 10 & 2 \\ \text{Paperback} \quad 8 & 13 & 7 \end{bmatrix} \end{array}$$

As Column Labels:

$$\begin{array}{c} & \text{Hardback} & \text{Paperback} \\ \text{Mysteries} & \begin{bmatrix} 5 & 8 \\ 10 & 13 \\ 2 & 7 \end{bmatrix} \\ \text{Science Fiction} \\ \text{History} \end{array}$$

Chapter 2

Algebra 1   31
Practice Workbook with Examples

NAME _____ DATE _____

Practice with Examples

For use with pages 86–91

Exercises for Example 1

1. Write and label a matrix to organize the following information.

Law Firm Personnel:
Males: 3 Attorneys, 4 Paralegals
Females: 4 Attorneys, 5 Paralegals

2. Write and label a matrix to organize the following information.

Car Rental Reservations:
Sedans: 26 budget, 47 luxury
Convertibles: 3 budget, 8 luxury
Sport Utility: 5 budget, 9 luxury

NAME _____ DATE _____

Practice with Examples
For use with pages 86–91

EXAMPLE 2 **Adding and Subtracting Matrices**

a. $\begin{bmatrix} 6 & -1 & 4 \\ 1 & 3 & 4 \end{bmatrix} + \begin{bmatrix} 5 & 0 & 1 \\ 8 & -4 & 3 \end{bmatrix} = \begin{bmatrix} 6+5 & -1+0 & 4+1 \\ 1+8 & 3+-4 & 4+3 \end{bmatrix}$

$= \begin{bmatrix} 11 & -1 & 5 \\ 9 & -1 & 7 \end{bmatrix}$

b. $\begin{bmatrix} -6 & 2 \\ -3 & -8 \end{bmatrix} - \begin{bmatrix} -1 & 0 \\ 4 & 7 \end{bmatrix} = \begin{bmatrix} -6-(-1) & 2-0 \\ -3-4 & -8-7 \end{bmatrix}$

$= \begin{bmatrix} -5 & 2 \\ -7 & -15 \end{bmatrix}$

c. $\begin{bmatrix} 1 & -3 \\ 4 & 6 \end{bmatrix} + \begin{bmatrix} 5 & -2 & 0 \\ 1 & -1 & 7 \end{bmatrix}$ The matrices cannot be added.

To add or subtract matrices, each matrix must have the same number of rows and columns.

Exercises for Example 2

3. Find the sum of the matrices.

$\begin{bmatrix} 9 & -3 \\ 0 & 3 \end{bmatrix} + \begin{bmatrix} -4 & -1 \\ 6 & 1 \end{bmatrix}$

4. Find the difference of the matrices.

$\begin{bmatrix} 1.5 & 0 \\ 3 & 2 \end{bmatrix} - \begin{bmatrix} 4 & -2.5 \\ -2 & -4 \end{bmatrix}$

Algebra 1
Practice Workbook with Examples

Chapter 2

NAME _____ DATE _____

Practice with Examples

For use with pages 93–98

GOAL Multiply real numbers using properties of multiplication and multiply real numbers to solve real-life problems

---

EXAMPLE 1 *Multiplying Real Numbers*

 a. $(0.5)(-26) = -13$ One negative factor

 b. $(-1)(-5)(-6) = -30$ Three negative factors

 c. $(-4)(6)\left(-\frac{1}{3}\right) = 8$ Two negative factors

Exercises for Example 1

Find the product.

 1. $(-2)(3)$

 2. $(-7)(-1)$

 3. $(10)(-2)$

 4. $(-12)(0.5)(-3)$

 5. $(-4)(-2)(-5)$

 6. $(6)(-6)(2)$

EXAMPLE 2 *Simplifying Variable Expressions*

 a. $(-2)(-7x) = 14x$ Two negative signs

 b. $-(y)^2 = -(y \cdot y) = -y^2$ One negative sign

Exercises for Example 2

Simplify the variable expression.

 7. $(5)(-w)$

 8. $8(-t)(-t)$

 9. $(-7)(-y)(-y)$

 10. $-\frac{1}{3}(6x)$

 11. $-4(a)(-a)(-a)$

 12. $-\frac{3}{5}(-s)(10s)$

NAME _____ DATE _____

Practice with Examples

For use with pages 93–98

EXAMPLE 3 *Evaluating a Variable Expression*

Evaluate the expression $(-12 \cdot x)(-3)$ when $x = -2$.

SOLUTION

$$(-12 \cdot x)(-3) = 36x \qquad \text{Simplify expression first.}$$
$$= 36(-2) \qquad \text{Substitute } -2 \text{ for } x.$$
$$= -72 \qquad \text{Simplify.}$$

Exercises for Example 3

Evaluate the expression.

13. $-15x$ when $x = 3$

14. $2p^2 - 3p$ when $p = -1$

15. $-4m^2 + 5m$ when $m = -2$

16. k^3 when $k = -3$

Practice with Examples

For use with pages 93–98

EXAMPLE 4 ***Using Multiplication in Real Life***

To promote its grand opening, a record store advertises compact discs for $10. The store loses $2.50 on each compact disc it sells. How much money will the store lose on its grand opening sale if it sells 256 discs?

SOLUTION

Multiply the number of discs sold by the loss per disc to find the total loss.

$$(256)(-2.50) = -640$$

The store loses $640 dollars on its grand opening sale.

Exercises for Example 4

17. Rework Example 4 if the store loses $1.50 on each disc.

18. Rework Example 4 if the store sells 185 discs.

Algebra 1
Practice Workbook with Examples

NAME _____ DATE _____

Practice with Examples

For use with pages 100–107

GOAL **Use the distributive property and simplify expressions by combining like terms**

VOCABULARY

In a term that is the product of a number and a variable, the number is the **coefficient** of the variable.

Like terms are terms that have the same variable raised to the same power. **Constant terms,** such as -3 and 5, are also like terms.

An expression is **simplified** if it has no grouping symbols and if all the like terms have been combined.

EXAMPLE 1 *Using the Distributive Property*

a. $-2(y - 3)$ $= -2(y) - (-2)(3)$ Distribute the -2.

                      $= -2y + 6$ Simplify.

b. $(-4n)(6 - n)$ $= (-4n)(6) - (-4n)(n)$ Distribute the $-4n$.

                          $= -24n + 4n^2$ Simplify.

Exercises for Example 1

Use the distributive property to rewrite the expression without parentheses.

1. $h(-3 - h)$ **2.** $(7 + 2y)(-3)$

3. $(-5q - 7)4$ **4.** $-6(s - 8)$

5. $-x(x + 1)$ **6.** $(-p + 2)(-5)$

Chapter 2

Practice with Examples

For use with pages 100–107

EXAMPLE 2 *Simplifying by Combining Like Terms*

a. $-11d + 5d$ $= (-11 + 5)d$ Use distributive property.

$= -6d$ Add coefficients.

b. $17s - 8 - 12s$ $= 17s - 12s - 8$ Group like terms.

$= 5s - 8$ Combine like terms.

Exercises for Example 2

Simplify the expression by combining like terms.

7. $20x + (-7x)$

8. $-y + 4y$

9. $3 + t^3 - 7$

10. $2n + 4 - n$

11. $-8a - 2a$

12. $10d - 3 + d$

Algebra 1
Practice Workbook with Examples

Chapter 2

NAME _____ DATE _____

Practice with Examples

For use with pages 100–107

EXAMPLE 3 *Using the Distributive Property to Combine Like Terms*

a. $7 - 3(2 + z) = 7 + (-3)(2 + z)$ Rewrite as an addition expression.

$= 7 + [(-3)(2) + (-3)(z)]$ Distribute the -3.

$= 7 + (-6) + (-3z)$ Multiply.

$= 1 - 3z$ Combine like terms and simplify.

b. $4x(5 - x) - 2x = 4x[5 + (-x)] - 2x$ Rewrite as an addition expression.

$= (4x)(5) + (4x)(-x) - 2x$ Distribute the $4x$.

$= 20x - 4x^2 - 2x$ Multiply.

$= 20x - 2x - 4x^2$ Group like terms.

$= 18x - 4x^2$ Combine like terms and simplify.

Exercises for Example 3

Apply the distributive property. Then simplify by combining like terms.

13. $(2w + 4)(-3) + w$ **14.** $3(5 - q) - q$

15. $-9t(t - 4) - 12$ **16.** $x^2 - 2x(x + 7)$

17. $-(6y - 5) + 6y$ **18.** $15d^2 + (2 - d)4d$

Chapter 2

Practice with Examples

For use with pages 108–113

GOAL   **Divide real numbers and use division to simplify algebraic expressions**

> ### VOCABULARY
>
> The product of a number and its **reciprocal** is 1.

EXAMPLE 1   *Dividing Real Numbers*

Find the quotient.

  a. $-30 \div 10$ **b.** $-24 \div (-6)$ **c.** $5 \div \left(-\frac{1}{3}\right)$

SOLUTION

  a. $-30 \div 10 \quad = -30 \cdot \frac{1}{10} = -3$

  b. $-24 \div (-6) \quad = -24 \cdot \left(-\frac{1}{6}\right) = 4$

  c. $5 \div \left(-\frac{1}{3}\right) \quad = 5(-3) = -15$

Exercises for Example 1

Find the quotient.

1. $36 \div (-3)$ **2.** $-28 \div (-7)$

3. $-13 \div 26$ **4.** $4 \div \left(-\frac{1}{2}\right)$

5. $-\frac{1}{3} \div (-5)$ **6.** $-25 \div 5$

Algebra 1
Practice Workbook with Examples

Chapter 2

NAME _____ DATE _____

Practice with Examples

For use with pages 108–113

EXAMPLE 2 *Using the Distributive Property to Simplify*

Simplify the expression $\dfrac{48x + 6}{6}$.

SOLUTION

$$\dfrac{48x + 6}{6}$$

$= (48x + 6) \div 6$	Rewrite fraction as division expression.
$= (48x + 6)\left(\frac{1}{6}\right)$	Multiply by reciprocal.
$= (48x)\left(\frac{1}{6}\right) + 6\left(\frac{1}{6}\right)$	Use distributive property.
$= 8x + 1$	Simplify.

Exercises for Example 2

Simplify the expression.

7. $\dfrac{-35 + 14y}{7}$

8. $\dfrac{28 - 7x}{-14}$

9. $\dfrac{18a + 30}{-3}$

Practice with Examples

For use with pages 108–113

EXAMPLE 3 *Evaluating an Expression*

Evaluate the expression $\dfrac{3c + d}{d}$ when $c = -4$ and $d = -2$.

SOLUTION

$$\frac{3c + d}{d} = \frac{3(-4) + (-2)}{-2} = \frac{-12 + (-2)}{-2} = \frac{-14}{-2} = 7$$

Exercises for Example 3

Evaluate the expression for the given value(s) of the variable(s).

10. $\dfrac{2m - 9}{3}$ when $m = 6$

11. $\dfrac{y - 2x}{x}$ when $y = 8$ and $x = 2$

12. $\dfrac{11 - q}{7}$ when $q = -3$

13. $\dfrac{5a + 2b}{a}$ when $a = -1$ and $b = -2$

Practice with Examples

For use with pages 114–120

GOAL Find the probability of an event and find the odds of an event

---

VOCABULARY

The **probability of an event** is the likelihood that the event will occur due to chance.

Outcomes are the different possible results of a probability experiment.

Favorable outcomes are the outcomes for the particular event you wish to have happen.

A **theoretical probability** is based on reasoning in which the *possible* outcomes are counted.

Experimental probability is based on the results of an experiment in which *actual* outcomes are counted.

The **odds** that an event will occur is the quotient of the number of favorable outcomes and the number of unfavorable outcomes.

EXAMPLE 1 *Finding the Probability of an Event*

You toss two coins. What is the probability that only one is heads?

SOLUTION

There are four possible outcomes that are equally likely. They are HH, HT, TH, and TT.

$$P = \frac{\text{Number of favorable outcomes}}{\text{Total number of outcomes}} = \frac{2}{4} = 0.5$$

The probability that only one is heads is 0.5.

Exercises for Example 1

In Exercises 1 and 2, find the probability of choosing a blue marble from a bag of blue and yellow marbles.

1. Number of blue marbles: 12

Total number of marbles: 48

2. Number of yellow marbles: 18

Total number of marbles: 50

Chapter 2

Practice with Examples

For use with pages 114–120

EXAMPLE 2 *Finding the Odds of an Event*

You randomly choose the letter A from a bag that contains the letters in the word ALABAMA. Find the odds of choosing the letter A.

SOLUTION

There are 4 favorable outcomes. There are 3 unfavorable outcomes.

$$\text{Odds} = \frac{\text{Number of favorable outcomes}}{\text{Number of unfavorable outcomes}} = \frac{4}{3}$$

The odds of choosing the letter A are 4 to 3.

Exercises for Example 2

Find the odds of choosing the indicated letter from a bag that contains the letters in the given word.

3. A; CANADA

4. N; ARGENTINA

5. S; RUSSIA

Chapter 2

NAME _____ DATE _____

Practice with Examples

EXAMPLE 3 *Finding Odds from Probability*

The probability that an event will occur is 0.43. What are the odds that
the event will occur?

SOLUTION

$$\text{Odds} \quad = \frac{\text{Probability event will occur}}{1 - (\text{Probability event will occur})}$$

$$= \frac{0.43}{1 - 0.43} \qquad\qquad \text{Substitute for probabilities.}$$

$$= \frac{0.43}{0.57} \qquad\qquad\quad \text{Simplify denominator.}$$

$$= \frac{43}{57} \qquad\qquad\quad\; \text{Multiply numerator and denominator by 100.}$$

The odds are 43 to 57 that the event will occur.

Exercises for Example 3

Use the given probability to find the odds.

6. The probability that an event will occur is 0.25.

7. The probability that an event will occur is 0.53.

Chapter 2

Practice with Examples

For use with pages 132–137

GOAL Solve linear equations using addition and subtraction and use linear equations to solve real-life problems

> **VOCABULARY**
>
> **Equivalent** equations have the same solutions.
>
> **Inverse operations** are two operations that undo each other, such as addition and subtraction.
>
> Each time you apply a transformation to an equation, you are writing a **solution step.**
>
> In a **linear equation,** the variable is raised to the *first* power and does not occur inside a square root symbol, an absolute value symbol, or in a denominator.

EXAMPLE 1 *Adding to Each Side*

Solve $y - 7 = -2$.

SOLUTION

To isolate y, you need to undo the subtraction by applying the inverse operation of adding 7.

$$y - 7 = -2 \qquad \text{Write original equation.}$$
$$y - 7 + 7 = -2 + 7 \qquad \text{Add 7 to each side.}$$
$$y = 5 \qquad \text{Simplify.}$$

The solution is 5. Check by substituting 5 for y in the original equation.

Exercises for Example 1

Solve the equation.

1. $t - 11 = 4$

2. $x - 2 = -3$

3. $5 = d - 8$

NAME _____ DATE _____

Practice with Examples

For use with pages 132–137

EXAMPLE 2 **Subtracting from Each Side**

Solve $q + 4 = -9$.

SOLUTION

To isolate q, you need to undo the addition by applying the inverse operation of subtracting 4.

$q + 4 = -9$ Write original equation.

$q + 4 - 4 = -9 - 4$ Subtract 4 from each side.

$q = -13$ Simplify.

The solution is -13. Check by substituting -13 for q in the original equation.

Exercises for Example 2

Solve the equation.

4. $s + 1 = -8$ **5.** $-6 + b = 10$ **6.** $6 = w + 12$

EXAMPLE 3 **Simplifying First**

Solve $x - (-3) = 10$.

SOLUTION

$x - (-3) = 10$ Write original equation.

$x + 3 = 10$ Simplify.

$x + 3 - 3 = 10 - 3$ Subtract 3 from each side.

$x = 7$ Simplify.

The solution is 7. Check by substituting 7 for x in the original equation.

Exercises for Example 3

Solve the equation.

7. $8 + z = 1$ **8.** $7 = k - 2$ **9.** $9 = a + (-5)$

Chapter 3

NAME _____ DATE _____

Practice with Examples

For use with pages 132–137

EXAMPLE 4 *Modeling a Real-Life Problem*

The original price of a bicycle was marked down $20 to a sale price of
$85. What was the original price?

SOLUTION

Original price (p) − Price reduction (20) = Sale Price(85)

Solve the equation $p - 20 = 85$.

$$p - 20 = 85 \qquad \text{Write real-life equation.}$$
$$p - 20 + 20 = 85 + 20 \qquad \text{Add 20 to each side.}$$
$$p = 105 \qquad \text{Simplify.}$$

The original price was $105. Check this in the statement of the problem.

Exercise for Example 4

10. After a sale, the price of a stereo was marked up $35 to a regular
price of $310. What was the sale price?

NAME _____ DATE _____

Reteaching with Practice

For use with pages 138–144

GOAL Solve linear equations using multiplication and division and use linear equations to solve real-life problems

---

VOCABULARY

Properties of equality are rules of algebra that can be used to isolate a variable in an equation.

EXAMPLE 1 *Dividing Each Side of an Equation*

Solve $7n = -35$.

SOLUTION

To isolate n, you need to undo the multiplication by applying the inverse operation of dividing by 7.

$$7n = -35 \qquad \text{Write original equation.}$$

$$\frac{7n}{7} = \frac{-35}{7} \qquad \text{Divide each side by 7.}$$

$$n = -5 \qquad \text{Simplify.}$$

The solution is -5. Check by substituting -5 for n in the original equation.

Exercises for Example 1

Solve the equation.

1. $-12x = 6$

2. $4 = 24y$

3. $-5z = -35$

Chapter 3

NAME _____ DATE _____

Reteaching with Practice

For use with pages 138–144

EXAMPLE 2 *Multiplying Each Side of an Equation*

Solve $-\frac{3}{4}t = 9$.

SOLUTION

To isolate t, you need to multiply by the reciprocal of the fraction.

$$-\frac{3}{4}t = 9 \qquad \text{Write original equation.}$$

$$\left(-\frac{4}{3}\right)\left(-\frac{3}{4}\right)t = \left(-\frac{4}{3}\right)9 \qquad \text{Multiply each side by } -\frac{4}{3}.$$

$$t = -12 \qquad \text{Simplify.}$$

The solution is -12. Check by substituting -12 for t in the original equation.

Exercises for Example 2

Solve the equation.

4. $\frac{1}{6}c = -2$

5. $\frac{f}{7} = 3$

6. $\frac{2}{3}q = 12$

Algebra 1
Chapter 3 Practice Workbook

Chapter 3

NAME _____ DATE _____

Reteaching with Practice

For use with pages 138–144

EXAMPLE 3 *Modeling a Real-Life Problem*

Write and solve an equation to find your average speed s on a plane flight. You flew 525 miles in 1.75 hours.

SOLUTION

Verbal Model | Speed of jet | · | Time | = | Distance |

Labels   Speed of jet $= s$ (miles per hour)
Time $= 1.75$ (hours)
Distance $= 525$ (miles)

Algebraic Model

$$s(1.75) = 525$$ Write algebraic model.

$$\frac{s(1.75)}{1.75} = \frac{525}{1.75}$$ Divide each side by 1.75.

$$s = 300$$ Simplify.

The speed s was 300 miles per hour. Check this in the statement of the problem.

Exercises for Example 3

7. Write and solve an equation to find your average speed in an airplane if you flew 800 miles in 2.5 hours.

8. Write and solve an equation to find your time in an airplane if you flew 1530 miles at a speed of 340 miles per hour.

NAME _____ DATE _____

Practice with Examples

For use with pages 145–152

GOAL Use two or more transformations to solve an equation and use multi-step equations to solve real-life problems

---

EXAMPLE 1 *Solving a Linear Equation*

Solve $-3x - 4 = 5$.

SOLUTION

To isolate the variable x, undo the subtraction and then the multiplication.

$$-3x - 4 = 5 \qquad \text{Write original equation.}$$
$$-3x - 4 + 4 = 5 + 4 \qquad \text{Add 4 to each side.}$$
$$-3x = 9 \qquad \text{Simplify.}$$
$$\frac{-3x}{-3} = \frac{9}{-3} \qquad \text{Divide each side by } -3.$$
$$x = -3 \qquad \text{Simplify.}$$

The solution is -3. Check this in the original equation.

Exercises for Example 1

Solve the equation.

1. $5y + 8 = -2$

2. $7 - 6m = 1$

3. $\dfrac{x}{4} - 1 = 5$

NAME _____ DATE _____

Practice with Examples

For use with pages 145–152

EXAMPLE 2 *Using the Distributive Property and Combining Like Terms*

Solve $y + 5(y + 3) = 33$.

SOLUTION

$y + 5(y + 3) = 33$	Write original equation.
$y + 5y + 15 = 33$	Use distributive property.
$6y + 15 = 33$	Combine like terms.
$6y + 15 - 15 = 33 - 15$	Subtract 15 from each side.
$6y = 18$	Simplify.
$\dfrac{6y}{6} = \dfrac{18}{6}$	Divide each side by 6.
$y = 3$	Simplify.

The solution is 3. Check this in the original equation.

Exercises for Example 2

Solve the equation.

4. $4x - 8 + x = 2$

5. $6 - (b + 1) = 9$

6. $10(z - 2) = 1 + 4$

Chapter 3

Practice with Examples

For use with pages 145–152

EXAMPLE 3 *Solving a Real-Life Problem*

The sum of the ages of two sisters is 25. The second sister's age is 5
more than three times the first sister's age n. Find the two ages.

SOLUTION

First sister's age (n) + Second sister's age $(3n + 5)$ = 25

Solve $n + (3n + 5) = 25$.

$n + (3n + 5) = 25$	Write real-life equation.
$4n + 5 = 25$	Combine like terms.
$4n + 5 - 5 = 25 - 5$	Subtract 5 from each side.
$4n = 20$	Simplify.
$\dfrac{4n}{4} = \dfrac{20}{4}$	Divide each side by 4.
$n = 5$	Simplify.

The first sister's age is 5. The second sister's age is $3(5) + 5 = 20$.

Exercises for Example 3

7. A parking garage charges $3 plus $1.50 per hour. You have $12 to spend for
parking. Write and solve an equation to find the number of hours that you
can park.

8. As a lifeguard, you earn $6 per day plus $2.50 per hour. Write and solve an
equation to find how many hours you must work to earn $16 in one day.

Practice with Examples

For use with pages 154–159

GOAL Collect variables on one side of an equation and use equations to solve real-life problems

---

VOCABULARY

An **identity** is a linear equation that is true for all values of the variable.

EXAMPLE 1 *Collecting Variables on One Side*

Solve $20 - 3x = 2x$.

SOLUTION

Think of $20 - 3x$ as $20 + (-3x)$. Since $2x$ is greater than $-3x$, collect the x-terms on the right side.

$20 - 3x = 2x$	Write original equation.
$20 - 3x + 3x = 2x + 3x$	Add $3x$ to each side.
$20 = 5x$	Simplify.
$\dfrac{20}{5} = \dfrac{5x}{5}$	Divide each side by 5.
$4 = x$	Simplify.

Exercises for Example 1

Solve the equation.

1. $5q = -7q + 6$

2. $14d - 6 = 17d$

3. $-y + 7 = -8y$

NAME _____ DATE _____

Practice with Examples

For use with pages 154–159

EXAMPLE 2 **Many Solutions or No Solution**

a. Solve $2x + 3 = 2x + 4$.   **b.** Solve $-(t + 5) = -t - 5$

SOLUTION

a.
$2x + 3 = 2x + 4$	Write original equation.
$2x + 3 - 3 = 2x + 4 - 3$	Subtract 3 from each side.
$2x = 2x + 1$	Simplify.
$0 = 1$	Subtract $2x$ from each side.

The original equation has no solution, because $0 \neq 1$ for any value of x.

b.
$-(t + 5) = -t - 5$	Write original equation.
$-t - 5 = -t - 5$	Use distributive property.
$-5 = -5$	Add t to each side.

All values of t are solutions, because $-5 = -5$ is always true. The original equation is an *identity*.

Exercises for Example 2

Solve the equation.

4. $9z - 3 = 9z$

5. $2(f - 7) = 2f - 14$

6. $n + 3 = -5n$

Algebra 1
Practice Workbook with Examples

NAME _____ DATE _____

Practice with Examples

For use with pages 154–159

EXAMPLE 3 *Solving Real-Life Problems*

A health club charges nonmembers $2 per day to swim and $5 per day for aerobics classes. Members pay a yearly fee of $200 plus $3 per day for aerobics classes. Write and solve an equation to find the number of days you must use the club to justify a yearly membership.

SOLUTION

Let n represent the number of days that you use the club. Then find the number of times for which the two plans would cost the same.

$2n + 5n = 200 + 3n$	Write real-life equation.
$7n = 200 + 3n$	Combine like terms.
$7n - 3n = 200 + 3n - 3n$	Subtract $3n$ from each side.
$4n = 200$	Simplify.
$\dfrac{4n}{4} = \dfrac{200}{4}$	Divide each side by 4.
$n = 50$	Simplify.

You must use the club 50 days to justify a yearly membership.

Exercises for Example 3

7. Rework Example 3 if nonmembers pay $3 per day to swim.

8. Rework Example 3 if members pay a yearly fee of $220.

Chapter 3

NAME _____ DATE _____

Practice with Examples

For use with pages 160–165

GOAL Draw a diagram to understand real-life problems and use a table to check your answers

EXAMPLE 1 *Drawing a Diagram*

The front page of your school newspaper is $11\frac{1}{4}$ inches wide. The left margin is 1 inch and the right margin is $1\frac{1}{2}$ inches. The space between the four columns is $\frac{1}{4}$ inch. Find the width of each column.

SOLUTION

The diagram shows that the page is made up of the width of the left margin, the width of the right margin, three spaces between the columns, and the four columns.

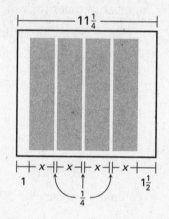

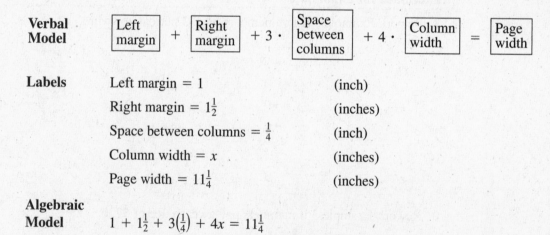

| Verbal Model | $\boxed{\text{Left margin}}$ | $+$ | $\boxed{\text{Right margin}}$ | $+\,3\cdot$ | $\boxed{\begin{array}{c}\text{Space between columns}\end{array}}$ | $+\,4\cdot$ | $\boxed{\begin{array}{c}\text{Column width}\end{array}}$ | $=$ | $\boxed{\begin{array}{c}\text{Page width}\end{array}}$ |

Labels   Left margin $= 1$ (inch)

Right margin $= 1\frac{1}{2}$ (inches)

Space between columns $= \frac{1}{4}$ (inch)

Column width $= x$ (inches)

Page width $= 11\frac{1}{4}$ (inches)

Algebraic Model $1 + 1\frac{1}{2} + 3\left(\frac{1}{4}\right) + 4x = 11\frac{1}{4}$

Solving for x, you find that each column can be 2 inches wide.

NAME _____ DATE _____

Practice with Examples

For use with pages 160–165

Exercise for Example 1

1. Rework Example 1 if the front page of the newspaper has three columns.

EXAMPLE 2 *Using a Table as a Check*

While on business, your mother drove 65 miles per hour in an automobile and traveled 260 miles per hour in an airplane. She drove twice as many hours as she flew and the total mileage for the trip was 780 miles. How many hours did she drive?

a. Using the verbal model below, write and solve an algebraic equation.

b. Make a table to check your solution.

$$\boxed{\text{Driving rate}} \cdot \boxed{\text{Driving time}} + \boxed{\text{Flying rate}} \cdot \boxed{\text{Flying time}} = \boxed{\text{Total distance}}$$

SOLUTION

a.

$65 \cdot 2x + 260 \cdot x = 780$	Write algebraic model.
$130x + 260x = 780$	Simplify.
$390x = 780$	Combine like terms.
$x = 2$	Divide each side by 390.

You find that $x = 2$ hours flying time; therefore, she drove $2x = 4$ hours.

b.

Flying time, x (in hours)	1	2	3	4
Flying distance (in miles)	260	520	780	1040
Driving time, 2x (in hours)	2	4	6	8
Driving distance (in miles)	130	260	390	520
Total distance (in miles)	390	780	1170	1560

From the table you can see that the total distance is 780 miles when the driving time is $2x = 4$ hours.

Algebra 1
Practice Workbook with Examples

Chapter 3

NAME _____ DATE _____

Practice with Examples

For use with pages 160–165

Exercise for Example 2

2. Rework Example 2 if she drove three times as many hours as she flew
and the total mileage for the trip was 1365 miles.

Chapter 3

NAME _____ DATE _____

Practice with Examples

For use with pages 166–172

GOAL **Find exact and approximate solutions of equations that contain decimals and solve real-life problems**

> **VOCABULARY**
>
> **Round-off error** occurs when you must use solutions that are not exact.

EXAMPLE 1 *Rounding for the Final Answer*

Solve $4.12x - 16.40 = 2.38x - 0.12$. Round the result to the nearest hundredth.

SOLUTION

$4.12x - 16.40 = 2.38x - 0.12$	Write original equation.
$1.74x - 16.40 = -0.12$	Subtract $2.38x$ from each side.
$1.74x = 16.28$	Add 16.40 to each side.
$x = \dfrac{16.28}{1.74}$	Divide each side by 1.74.
$x = 9.35632. . .$	Use a calculator.
$x \approx 9.36$	Round to the nearest hundredth.

The solution is approximately 9.36.

Exercises for Example 1
....

Solve the equation. Round the result to the nearest hundredth.

1. $7.23x + 16.51 = 47.89 - 2.55x$ **2.** $6.6(1.2 - 7.3x) = 16.4x + 5.8$

3. $-4(5.4y - 37.2) = 9.7$ **4.** $0.34b - 5.20 = 0.15b - 8.88$

Chapter 3

NAME _____ DATE _____

Practice with Examples

For use with pages 166–172

EXAMPLE 2 *Changing Decimal Coefficients to Integers*

Multiply the equation by a power of 10 to write an equivalent equation with integer coefficients. Solve the equivalent equation and round to the nearest hundredth.

$$3.11x - 17.64 = 2.02x - 5.89$$

SOLUTION

$3.11x - 17.64 = 2.02x - 5.89$	Write original equation.
$311x - 1764 = 202x - 589$	Multiply each side by 100.
$109x - 1764 = -589$	Subtract $202x$ from each side.
$109x = 1175$	Add 1764 to each side.
$x = \frac{1175}{109}$	Divide each side by 109.
$x = 10.77981. . .$	Use a calculator.
$x \approx 10.78$	Round to nearest hundredth.

The solution is approximately 10.78. Check this in the original equation.

Exercises for Example 2

Multiply the equation by a power of 10 to write an equivalent equation with integer coefficients. Then solve the equivalent equation and round to the nearest hundredth.

5. $5.8 + 3.2x = 3.4x - 16.7$

6. $-0.83y + 0.17 = 0.72y$

Chapter 3

NAME _____ DATE _____

Practice with Examples

For use with pages 166–172

EXAMPLE 3 *Using a Verbal Model*

While dining at a restaurant, you want to leave a 15% tip. You have a total of $14.00 to spend. What is your price limit for the dinner plus a tip? Using the verbal model below, write and solve an algebraic equation.

$$\boxed{\text{Price limit}} \ + \ \boxed{\text{Tip rate}} \ \cdot \ \boxed{\text{Price limit}} \ = \ \boxed{\text{Total cost}}$$

SOLUTION

Let x represent your price limit.

$x + 0.15x = 14.00$	Write algebraic model.
$1.15x = 14.00$	Combine like terms.
$x = \dfrac{14.00}{1.15}$	Divide each side by 1.15.
$x = 12.173913\ldots$	Use a calculator.
$x \approx 12.17$	Round down.

The answer is rounded *down* to $12.17 because you have a limited amount to spend.

Exercises for Example 3

7. Rework Example 3 if you have $16.00 to spend.

8. Rework Example 3 if you want to leave a 20% tip.

Algebra 1
Practice Workbook with Examples

Practice with Examples

For use with pages 174–179

 GOAL Solve a formula or literal equation for one of its variables and rewrite an equation in function form

---

VOCABULARY

A **formula** is an algebraic equation that relates two or more real-life quantities.

A two-variable equation is written in **function form** if one of its variables is isolated on one side of the equation.

EXAMPLE 1 *Solving and Using an Area Formula*

Use the formula for the area of a rectangle, $A = lw$.

a. Solve the formula for the width w.

b. Use the new formula to find the width of a rectangle that has an area of 72 square inches and a length of 9 inches.

SOLUTION

a. Solve for width w.

$A = lw$ Write original formula.

$\dfrac{A}{l} = \dfrac{lw}{l}$ To isolate w, divide each side by l.

$\dfrac{A}{l} = w$ Simplify.

b. Substitute the given values into the new formula.

$$w = \frac{A}{l} = \frac{72}{9} = 8$$

The width of the rectangle is 8 inches.

NAME _____ DATE _____

Practice with Examples

For use with pages 174–179

Exercises for Example 1

Solve for the indicated variable.

1. Area of a Triangle

Solve for h: $A = \frac{1}{2}bh$

2. Circumference of a Circle

Solve for r: $C = 2\pi r$

3. Simple Interest

Solve for P: $I = Prt$

4. Simple Interest

Solve for r: $I = Prt$

EXAMPLE 2 *Rewriting an Equation in Function Form*

a. Rewrite the equation $19 - 3y = 8x - 2x + 10$ so that y is a function of x.

b. Use the result to find y when $x = -2, -1, 0,$ and 1.

SOLUTION

a.

$19 - 3y = 8x - 2x + 10$	Write original equation.
$19 - 3y = 6x + 10$	Combine like terms.
$19 - 19 - 3y = 6x + 10 - 19$	Subtract 19 from each side.
$-3y = 6x - 9$	Simplify.
$\dfrac{-3y}{-3} = \dfrac{6x - 9}{-3}$	Divide each side by -3.
$y = -2x + 3$	Simplify.

The equation $y = -2x + 3$ represents y as a function of x.

b.

INPUT		SUBSTITUTE		OUTPUT
$x = -2$	Substitute	$y = -2(-2) + 3$	Simplify	$y = 7$
$x = -1$	Substitute	$y = -2(-1) + 3$	Simplify	$y = 5$
$x = 0$	Substitute	$y = -2(0) + 3$	Simplify	$y = 3$
$x = 1$	Substitute	$y = -2(1) + 3$	Simplify	$y = 1$

Chapter 3

NAME _____ DATE _____

Practice with Examples

For use with pages 174–179

Exercises for Example 2

Rewrite each equation so that *y* is a function of *x*. Then use the result to find *y* when *x* = −2, −1, 0, and 1.

5. $-7x + y = 8$

6. $6y - 3x = 12$

7. $20x = 4y - 4$

Algebra 1
Practice Workbook with Examples

Practice with Examples

For use with pages 180–185

GOAL **Use rates, ratios, and percents to model and solve real-life problems**

> **VOCABULARY**
>
> If a and b are two quantities measured in different units, then the **rate of a per b** is $\frac{a}{b}$.
>
> A **unit rate** is a rate per one given unit.

EXAMPLE 1 *Finding a Unit Rate*

While visiting Italy you want to exchange $120 for liras. The rate of currency exchange is 1850 liras per United States dollar. How many liras will you receive?

SOLUTION

You can use unit analysis to write an equation.

$$\text{dollars} \cdot \frac{\text{liras}}{\text{dollars}} = \text{liras}$$

$$D \cdot \frac{1850}{1} = L \qquad \text{Write equation.}$$

$$120 \cdot \frac{1850}{1} = L \qquad \text{Substitute 120 for } D \text{ dollars.}$$

$$222{,}000 = L \qquad \text{Simplify.}$$

You will receive 222,000 liras.

Exercises for Example 1
....
Convert the currency using the given exchange rate.

1. Convert $150 U.S. dollars to German marks. ($1 U.S. is 1.8943 marks)

2. Convert $200 U.S. dollars to Austrian schillings. ($1 U.S. is 13.3272 schillings)

NAME _____ DATE _____

Practice with Examples

For use with pages 180–185

EXAMPLE 2 **Using Ratios to Write an Equation**

You took a survey of your classmates and found that 9 of the 27 classmates have public library cards. Use your results to make a prediction for the 855 students enrolled in your school.

SOLUTION

You can answer the question by writing a ratio. Let n represent the number of students in your school that have public library cards.

$$\frac{\text{Library cards in sample}}{\text{Total students in sample}} = \frac{\text{Library cards in school}}{\text{Total students in school}}$$

$$\frac{9}{27} = \frac{n}{855} \qquad\qquad \text{Write equation.}$$

$$855 \cdot \frac{9}{27} = n \qquad\qquad \text{Multiply each side by 855.}$$

$$285 = n \qquad\qquad \text{Simplify.}$$

Of the 855 students enrolled in the school, about 285 will have a public library card.

Exercises for Example 2

3. Rework Example 2 if 6 of the 27 classmates have public library cards.

4. Rework Example 2 if 930 students are enrolled in the school.

Chapter 3

NAME _____ DATE _____

Practice with Examples

For use with pages 180–185

EXAMPLE 3 *Finding Percents*

What percent was the waiter's tip if he received $3.60 for a $20.00 meal?

SOLUTION

To find the percent, divide the amount of the tip by the price of the meal.

$\dfrac{3.60}{20.00} = 0.18$, so the tip was 18% of the price of the meal.

Exercises for Example 3

Find the percent. Round to the nearest whole percent.

5. Tax of $2.88 on an item priced at $36

6. $3 tip on a meal priced at $16

Chapter 3

NAME _____ DATE _____

Practice with Examples

For use with pages 203–208

GOAL **Plot points in a coordinate plane, draw a scatter plot, and make predictions about real-life situations**

VOCABULARY

A **coordinate plane** is formed by two real number lines that intersect at a right angle.

Each point in a coordinate plane corresponds to an **ordered pair** of real numbers. The first number is the **x-coordinate** and the second number is the **y-coordinate.**

A **scatter plot** is a graph containing several points that represent real-life data.

EXAMPLE 1 *Plotting Points in a Coordinate Plane*

Plot and label the following ordered pairs in a coordinate plane.

a. $(3, -2)$ **b.** $(-4, 3)$

SOLUTION

To plot a point, you move along the horizontal and vertical lines in the coordinate plane and mark the location that corresponds to the ordered pair.

a. To plot the point $(3, -2)$, start at the origin. Move 3 units to the right and 2 units down.

b. To plot the point $(-4, 3)$, start at the origin. Move 4 units to the left and 3 units up.

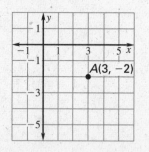   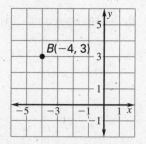

Exercises for Example 1

Plot and label the ordered pairs in a coordinate plane.

1. $A(5, 4), B(-3, 0), C(-1, -2)$ **2.** $A(-3, 2), B(0, 0), C(2, -2)$

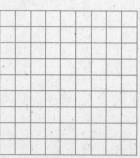   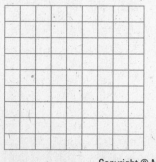

Algebra 1
Practice Workbook with Examples

LESSON
4.1
CONTINUED

NAME _____ DATE _____

Practice with Examples

For use with pages 203–208

3. $A(0, -4), B(3, 5), C(3, -1)$

4. $A(-1, -2), B(5, -2), C(-4, 0)$

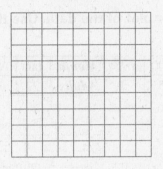

5. $A(-1, 3), B(2, 0), C(3, -2)$

6. $A(2, 4), B(-2, 5), C(0, 3)$

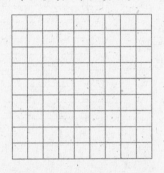

EXAMPLE 2 ### *Sketching a Scatter Plot*

The table below gives the U.S. postal rates (in cents) for first-class mail, based on the weight (in ounces) of the mail. Draw a scatter plot of the data and predict the postal rate for a piece of mail that weighs 8 ounces.

Weight (ounces)	1	2	3	4	5
Rate (cents)	33	55	77	99	121

SOLUTION

❶ Rewrite the data in the table as a list of ordered pairs.

$(1, 33), (2, 55), (3, 77), (4, 99), (5, 121)$

❷ Draw a coordinate plane. Put weight w on the horizontal axis and rate r on the vertical axis.

❸ Plot the points.

❹ From the scatter plot, you can see that the points follow a pattern. By extending the pattern, you can predict that the postal rate for an 8 ounce piece of mail is about 187 cents, or $1.87.

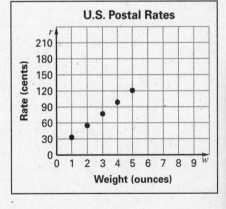

Chapter 4

NAME _____ DATE _____

Practice with Examples

For use with pages 203–208

Exercises for Example 2

In Exercises 7 and 8, make a scatter plot of the data. Use the horizontal axis to represent time.

7.

Year	1997	1998	1999	2000
Members	74	81	89	95

8.

Month	Jan.	Apr.	Aug.	Dec.
Adults	22	30	15	42

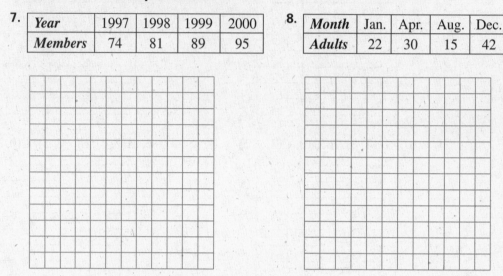

In Exercises 9 and 10, use a scatter plot to see if the given information is correct. If not, explain how the data should be changed. Use the horizontal axis to represent quarts in Exercise 9 and hours in Exercise 10.

9.

Quarts	3.0	4.0	5.0	6.0
Gallons	0.75	1.0	1.3	1.5

10.

Hours	3	5	6	8
Rental charge (dollars)	14	20	24	32

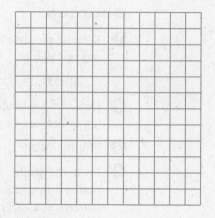

NAME _____ DATE _____

Practice with Examples

For use with pages 210–217

GOAL Graph a linear equation using a table or a list of values and graph horizontal and vertical lines

> ### VOCABULARY
>
> A **solution of an equation** in two variables x and y is an ordered pair (x, y) that makes the equation true.
>
> The **graph of an equation** in x and y is the set of all points (x, y) that are solutions of the equation.

EXAMPLE 1 *Verifying Solutions of an Equation*

Use algebra to decide whether the point $(10, 1)$ lies on the graph of $x - 2y = 8$.

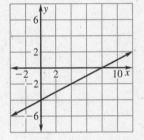

SOLUTION

The point $(10, 1)$ appears to be on the graph of $x - 2y = 8$. You can check this algebraically.

$$x - 2y = 8 \qquad \text{Write original equation.}$$
$$10 - 2(1) \overset{?}{=} 8 \qquad \text{Substitute 10 for } x \text{ and 1 for } y.$$
$$8 = 8 \qquad \text{Simplify. True statement}$$

$(10, 1)$ is a solution of the equation $x - 2y = 8$, so it is on the graph.

Exercises for Example 1

Decide whether the given ordered pair is a solution of the equation.

1. $-3x + 6y = 12, (-4, 0)$

2. $x + 5y = 11, (2, 1)$

3. $y = 1, (3, 1)$

4. $3y - 5x = 4, (-2, 2)$

Practice with Examples

For use with pages 210–217

EXAMPLE 2 *Graphing a Linear Equation*

Use a table of values to graph the equation $x - 2y = 4$.

SOLUTION

Rewrite the equation in function form by solving for y.

$x - 2y = 4$	Write original equation.
$-2y = -x + 4$	Subtract x from each side.
$y = \dfrac{x}{2} - 2$	Divide each side by -2.

Choose a variety of values of x and make a table of values.

Choose x.	-4	-2	0	2	4
Evaluate y.	-4	-3	-2	-1	0

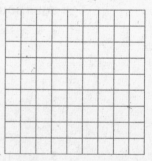

Using the table of values, you can write five ordered pairs.

$(-4, -4), (-2, -3), (0, -2), (2, -1), (4, 0)$

Plot each ordered pair. The line through the points is the graph of the equation.

Exercises for Example 2

Use a table of values to graph the equation.

5. $y = 3x - 4$ **6.** $3y - 3x = 6$ **7.** $y = -3(x - 1)$

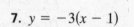

NAME _____ DATE _____

Practice with Examples

For use with pages 210–217

EXAMPLE 3 *Graphing y = b*

Graph the equation $y = -3$.

SOLUTION

The y-value is always -3, regardless of the value of x. The points $(-1, -3)$, $(0, -3)$, $(2, -3)$ are some solutions of the equation. The graph of the equation is a horizontal line 3 units below the x-axis.

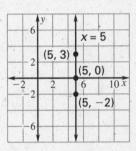

EXAMPLE 4 *Graphing x = a*

Graph the equation $x = 5$.

SOLUTION

The x-value is always 5, regardless of the value of y. The points $(5, -2)$, $(5, 0)$, $(5, 3)$ are some solutions of the equation. The graph of the equation is a vertical line 5 units to the right of the y-axis.

Exercises for Examples 3 and 4

Graph the equation.

8. $y = 0$

9. $x = -4$

10. $x = 0$

11. $y = 6$

12. $y = -5$

13. $x = 2$

Algebra 1
Practice Workbook with Examples

NAME _____ DATE _____

Practice with Examples

For use with pages 218–224

GOAL Find the intercepts of the graph of a linear equation and use the intercepts to sketch a quick graph of a linear equation

---

VOCABULARY

An **x-intercept** is the x-coordinate of a point where a graph crosses the x-axis. The y-coordinate of this point is 0.

A **y-intercept** is the y-coordinate of a point where a graph crosses the y-axis. The x-coordinate of this point is 0.

EXAMPLE 1 *Finding Intercepts*

Find the x-intercept and the y-intercept of the graph of the equation $4x - 2y = 8$.

SOLUTION

To find the x-intercept of $4x - 2y = 8$, let $y = 0$.

$$4x - 2y = 8 \qquad \text{Write original equation.}$$
$$4x - 2(0) = 8 \qquad \text{Substitute 0 for } y.$$
$$x = 2 \qquad \text{Solve for } x.$$

The x-intercept is 2. The line crosses the x-axis at the point $(2, 0)$.

To find the y-intercept of $4x - 2y = 8$, let $x = 0$.

$$4x - 2y = 8 \qquad \text{Write original equation.}$$
$$4(0) - 2y = 8 \qquad \text{Substitute 0 for } x.$$
$$y = -4 \qquad \text{Solve for } y.$$

The y-intercept is -4. The line crosses the y-axis at the point $(0, -4)$.

Chapter 4

NAME _____ DATE _____

Practice with Examples

For use with pages 218–224

Exercises for Example 1

Find the *x*-intercept of the graph of the equation.

1. $x - y = 6$ **2.** $-2x + y = -4$ **3.** $3x - 2y = 6$

Find the *y*-intercept of the graph of the equation.

4. $x - y = 6$ **5.** $-2x + y = -4$ **6.** $3x - 2y = 6$

EXAMPLE 2 *Making a Quick Graph*

Graph the equation $2x - y = 8$.

SOLUTION

Find the intercepts by first substituting 0 for *y* and then substituting 0 for *x*.

$$2x - y = 8 \qquad\qquad 2x - y = 8$$
$$2x - 0 = 8 \qquad\qquad 2(0) - y = 8$$
$$2x = 8 \qquad\qquad\qquad -y = 8$$
$$x = 4 \qquad\qquad\qquad\; y = -8$$

The *x*-intercept is 4.   The *y*-intercept is -8.

Draw a coordinate plane that includes the points $(4, 0)$ and $(0, -8)$. Plot the points $(4, 0)$ and $(0, -8)$ and draw a line through them. The graph is shown below.

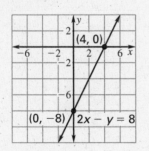

NAME _____ DATE _____

Practice with Examples

For use with pages 218–224

Exercises for Example 2

Find the x-intercept and the y-intercept of the line. Use the intercepts to sketch a quick graph of the equation.

7. $y = -x + 6$ **8.** $x - 5y = 15$ **9.** $y = 4 - 2x$

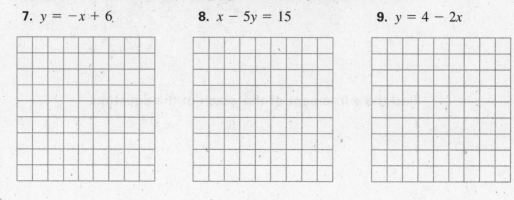

10. $7x - y = 14$ **11.** $3x + 4y = 24$ **12.** $2y = 7x + 10$

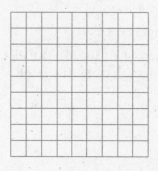
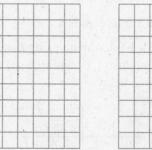

Algebra 1
Practice Workbook with Examples

NAME _____ DATE _____

Practice with Examples

For use with pages 226–233

GOAL **Find the slope of a line using two of its points and how to interpret slope as a rate of change in real-life situations**

VOCABULARY

The **slope** m of a nonvertical line is the number of units the line rises or falls for each unit of horizontal change from left to right.

A **rate of change** compares two different quantities that are changing.

EXAMPLE 1 *Finding the Slope of a Line*

Find the slope of the line passing through $(-3, 2)$ and $(1, 5)$.

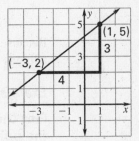

SOLUTION

Let $(x_1, y_1) = (-3, 2)$ and $(x_2, y_2) = (1, 5)$.

$$m = \frac{y_2 - y_1}{x_2 - x_1} \quad \leftarrow \text{ Rise: Difference of } y\text{-values}$$
$$\phantom{m = \frac{y_2 - y_1}{x_2 - x_1}} \quad \leftarrow \text{ Run: Difference of } x\text{-values}$$

$$= \frac{5 - 2}{1 - (-3)} \quad \text{Substitute values.}$$

$$= \frac{3}{1 + 3} = \frac{3}{4} \quad \text{Simplify. Slope is positive.}$$

Because the slope in Example 1 is positive, the line rises from left to right. If a line has negative slope, then the line falls from left to right.

Exercises for Example 1

Plot the points and find the slope of the line passing through them.

1. $(-4, 0), (3, 3)$ **2.** $(-1, -2), (2, -6)$ **3.** $(-3, -1), (1, 3)$

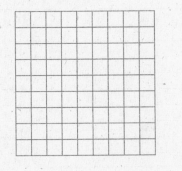 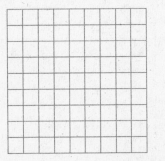 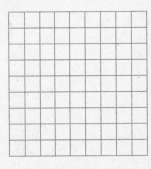

Chapter 4

NAME _____ DATE _____

Practice with Examples

For use with pages 226–233

EXAMPLE 2 *Finding the Slope of a Line*

Find the slope of the line passing through $(-4, 2)$ and $(1, 2)$.

SOLUTION

Let $(x_1, y_1) = (-4, 2)$ and $(x_2, y_2) = (1, 2)$.

$$m = \frac{y_2 - y_1}{x_2 - x_1} \qquad \leftarrow \text{ Rise: Difference of } y\text{-values}$$
$$\leftarrow \text{ Run: Difference of } x\text{-values}$$

$$= \frac{2 - 2}{1 - (-4)} \qquad \text{Substitute values.}$$

$$= \frac{0}{5} = 0 \qquad \text{Simplify. Slope is zero.}$$

Because the slope in Example 2 is zero, the line is horizontal. If the slope of a line is undefined, the line is vertical.

Exercises for Example 2

Plot the points and find the slope of the line passing through the points.

4. $(-4, 0), (-4, 3)$

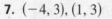

5. $(1, -1), (1, 3)$

6. $(-3, 0), (1, 0)$

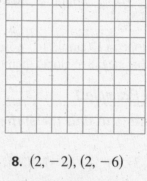

7. $(-4, 3), (1, 3)$

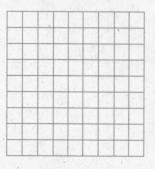

8. $(2, -2), (2, -6)$

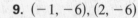

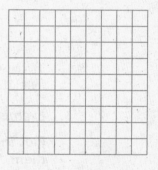

9. $(-1, -6), (2, -6)$

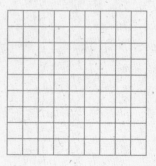

NAME _____ DATE _____

Practice with Examples

For use with pages 226–233

EXAMPLE 3 *Interpreting Slope as a Rate of Change*

In 1994, a video store had 23,500 rentals. In 2000, the store had 28,540 rentals. Find the average rate of change of the store's rentals in rentals per year.

SOLUTION

Use the formula for slope to find the average rate of change. The change in rentals is 28,540 − 23,500 = 5040 rentals. Subtract in the same order. The change in time is 2000 − 1994 = 6 years.

VERBAL MODEL	$\boxed{\text{Average rate of change}} = \dfrac{\boxed{\text{Change in rentals}}}{\boxed{\text{Change in time}}}$

LABELS   Average rate of change = m (rentals per year)
Change in rentals = 5040   (rentals)
Change in time = 6   (years)

ALGEBRAIC MODEL $m = \dfrac{5040}{6}$

The average rate of change is 840 rentals per year.

Exercises for Example 3

10. In 1992, the population of Seoul, South Korea was 17,334,000. In 1995, the population of Seoul was 19,065,000. Find the average rate of change of the population in people per year.

11. In 1990, the number of motorcycles registered in the United States was 4.3 million. In 1996, the number of registered motorcycles was 3.8 million. Find the average rate of change of the number of registered motorcycles in motorcycles per year.

NAME _____ DATE _____

Practice with Examples

For use with pages 234–239

GOAL Write linear equations that represent direct variation and use a ratio to write an equation for direct variation

---

VOCABULARY

In the model for direct variation $y = kx$, the nonzero number k is the **constant of variation**.

Two quantities that vary directly are said to have **direct variation**.

EXAMPLE 1 *Writing a Direct Variation Equation*

The variables x and y vary directly. When $x = 4$, $y = 6$.

a. Write an equation that relates x and y.

b. Find the value of y when $x = 12$.

SOLUTION

a. Because x and y vary directly, the equation is of the form $y = kx$. You can solve for k as follows.

$$y = kx \qquad \text{Write model for direct variation.}$$
$$6 = k(4) \qquad \text{Substitute 4 for } x \text{ and 6 for } y.$$
$$1.5 = k \qquad \text{Divide each side by 4.}$$

An equation that relates x and y is $y = 1.5x$.

b. $y = 1.5(12) \qquad$ Substitute 12 for x in $y = 1.5x$.
   $\quad\ y = 18 \qquad\qquad$ Simplify.

When $x = 12$, $y = 18$.

Exercises for Example 1
....

In Exercises 1–6, the variables x and y vary directly. Use the given values to write an equation that relates x and y.

1. $x = 3$, $y = 15$ 　　　　**2.** $x = 6$, $y = 3$ 　　　　**3.** $x = -4$, $y = -4$

4. $x = 10$, $y = -2$ 　　　**5.** $x = 3.5$, $y = 7$ 　　　**6.** $x = -12$, $y = 4$

Algebra 1
Practice Workbook with Examples

Practice with Examples

For use with pages 234–239

EXAMPLE 2 *Using a Ratio to Write a Model*

Weight varies directly with gravity. A person who weighs 150 pounds on Earth weighs 57 pounds on Mars.

a. Write a model that relates a person's weight E on Earth to that person's weight M on Mars.

b. A person weighs 210 pounds on Earth. Use the model to estimate that person's weight on Mars.

SOLUTION

a. Rewrite the model $E = kM$ for direct variation as $k = \dfrac{E}{M}$.

This is the ratio form of a direct variation model. When $E = 150$ and $M = 57$, $k = \dfrac{150}{57}$. The model for direct variation is $E = \dfrac{150}{57}M$.

b. Use the model $E = \dfrac{150}{57}M$ to estimate the person's weight on Mars.

$$210 = \frac{150}{57}M \qquad \text{Substitute 210 for } E.$$

$$79.8 \approx M \qquad \text{Multiply each side by } \frac{57}{150}.$$

You estimate that the person weighs about 79.8 pounds on Mars.

NAME _____ DATE _____

Practice with Examples

For use with pages 234–239

Exercises for Example 2

7. Use the ratio model $E = \frac{150}{57}M$ to estimate a person's weight on Mars if the person weighs 120 pounds on Earth.

8. Use the ratio model $E = \frac{150}{57}M$ to estimate a person's weight on Earth if the person weighs 62 pounds on Mars.

9. A person who weighs 160 pounds on Earth weighs 139 pounds on Venus.
   a. Write a model that relates a person's weight E on Earth to that person's weight V on Venus.

   b. A person weighs 195 pounds on Earth. Use the model to estimate that person's weight on Venus.

NAME _____ DATE _____

Practice with Examples

For use with pages 241–247

GOAL Graph a linear equation in slope-intercept form and interpret equations in slope-intercept form

---

VOCABULARY

The linear equation $y = mx + b$ is written in **slope-intercept form.** The slope of the line is m. The y-intercept is b.

Two different lines in the same plane are **parallel** if they do not intersect. Any two nonvertical lines are parallel if and only if they have the same slope (all vertical lines are parallel).

EXAMPLE 1 *Writing Equations in Slope-Intercept Form*

EQUATION	SLOPE-INTERCEPT FORM	SLOPE	y-INTERCEPT
a. $y = 3x$	$y = 3x + 0$	$m = 3$	$b = 0$
b. $y = \dfrac{2x - 3}{5}$	$y = \dfrac{2}{5}x - \dfrac{3}{5}$	$m = \dfrac{2}{5}$	$b = -\dfrac{3}{5}$
c. $4x + 8y = 24$	$y = -0.5x + 3$	$m = -0.5$	$b = 3$

Exercises for Example 1

Write the equation in slope-intercept form. Find the slope and the y-intercept

1. $y = -3x$

2. $x + y - 5 = 0$

3. $3x + y = 5$

4. $y = \dfrac{-x + 7}{3}$

5. $y = 2$

6. $x + 4y - 4 = 0$

7. Which two lines in Exercises 1–6 are parallel? Explain.

NAME _____ DATE _____

Practice with Examples

For use with pages 241–247

EXAMPLE 2 **Graphing Using Slope and y-Intercept**

Graph the equation $5x - y = 3$.

SOLUTION

Write the equation in slope-intercept form: $y = 5x - 3$

Find the slope and the y-intercept: $m = 5$ and $b = -3$.

Plot the point $(0, b)$. Draw a slope triangle to locate
a second point on the line.

$$m = \frac{5}{1} = \frac{\text{rise}}{\text{run}}$$

Draw a line through the two

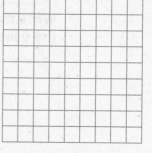

Exercises for Example 2

**Write the equation in slope-intercept form. Then graph the
equation.**

8. $6x - y = 0$ **9.** $x + 3y - 3 = 0$ **10.** $5x + y = 4$

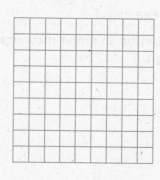
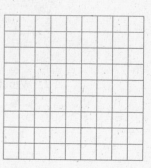

11. $x + 3y - 6 = 0$ **12.** $2x + y - 9 = 0$ **13.** $x + 2y + 8 = 0$

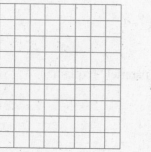
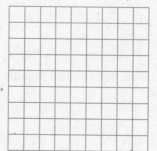

Chapter 4

NAME _____ DATE _____

Practice with Examples

For use with pages 241–247

EXAMPLE 3 *Using Slope-Intercept Form to Solve a Real-Life Problem*

During the summer you work for a lawn care service. You are paid $5 per day, plus an hourly rate of $1.50.

a. Using w to represent daily wages and h to represent the number of hours worked daily, write an equation that models your total wages for one day's work.

b. Find the slope and the y-intercept of the equation.

c. What does the slope represent?

d. Graph the equation, using the slope and the y-intercept.

SOLUTION

a. Using w to represent daily wages and h to represent the number of hours worked daily, the equation that models your total wages for one day's work is $w = 1.50h + 5$.

b. The slope of the equation is 1.50 and the y-intercept is 5.

c. The slope represents the hourly rate.

d.

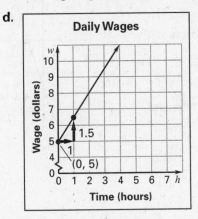

Exercises for Example 3

14. Rework Example 3 if you are paid $4 per day, plus an hourly rate of $1.75.

15. Rework Example 3 if you are paid $6 per day, plus an hourly rate of $1.25.

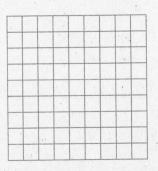

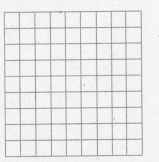

NAME _____ DATE _____

Practice with Examples

For use with pages 250–255

GOAL **Solve a linear equation graphically and use a graph to approximate solutions in real-life problems**

The first step in solving a linear equation graphically is to write the equation in the form $ax + b = 0$. Next, write the related function $y = ax + b$. Finally, graph the equation $y = ax + b$. The solution of $ax + b = 0$ is the x-intercept of $y = ax + b$.

EXAMPLE 1 *Solving an Equation Graphically*

Solve $3x - 1 = 5$ graphically. Check your solution algebraically.

SOLUTION

❶ Write the equation in the form $ax + b = 0$.

| $3x - 1 = 5$ | Write original equation. |
| $3x - 6 = 0$ | Subtract 5 from each side. |

❷ Write the related function $y = 3x - 6$.

❸ Graph the equation $y = 3x - 6$.
   The x-intercept appears to be 2.

❹ Use substitution to check your solution.

$$3x - 1 = 5$$
$$3(2) - 1 \overset{?}{=} 5$$
$$6 - 1 = 5 \qquad \leftarrow \text{True statement}$$

The solution of $3x - 1 = 5$ is 2.

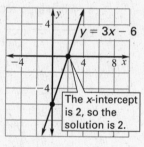

The x-intercept is 2, so the solution is 2.

Practice with Examples

For use with pages 250–255

Exercises for Example 1

Solve the equation graphically. Check your solution algebraically.

1. $5x + 2 = 7$

2. $-3x = 15$

3. $2 - x = 5$

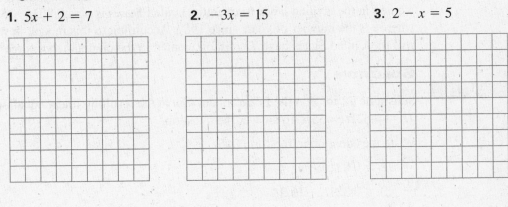

4. $8 + 2x = -2x$

5. $0.5x + 1 = 3$

6. $3x + 6 = 11 - 2x$

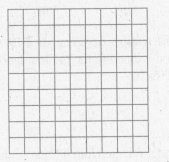
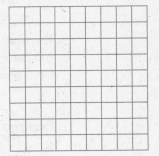

Practice with Examples

For use with pages 250–255

EXAMPLE 2 *Approximating a Real-Life Solution*

Based on data from 1989 to 1995, a model for the number n (in millions) of women in the civilian labor force in the United States is $n = 0.821t + 55.7$, where t is the number of years since 1989. According to this model, in what year will the United States have 72 million women in the civilian labor force?

SOLUTION

Substitute 72 for n in the linear model. Solve the resulting linear equation, $72 = 0.821t + 55.7$, to answer the question.

Write the equation in the form $ax + b = 0$.

$$72 = 0.821t + 55.7$$

$$0 = 0.821t - 16.3$$

Graph the related function $n = 0.821t - 16.3$.

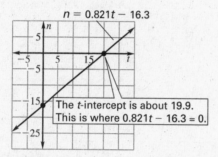

The t-intercept is about 19.9.
This is where $0.821t - 16.3 = 0$.

The t-intercept is about 19.9. Because t is the number of years since 1989, you can estimate that there will be 72 million women in the civilian labor force about 20 years after 1989, or about 2009.

Exercise for Example 2

7. Based on data from 1992 to 1995, a model for the United States consumer price index n is $n = 4t + 140.35$, where t is the number of years since 1992. According to this model, in what year will the United States have a consumer price index of 180.4?

Algebra 1
Practice Workbook with Examples

NAME _____ DATE _____

Practice with Examples

For use with pages 256–262

GOAL Identify when a relation is a function and use function notation to represent real-life situations

---

VOCABULARY

A **relation** is any set of ordered pairs. A relation is a function if for each input there is exactly one output.

Using **function notation,** the equation $y = 3x - 4$ becomes the function $f(x) = 3x - 4$ (the symbol $f(x)$ replaces y). Just as (x, y) is a solution of $y = 3x - 4$, $(x, f(x))$ is a solution of $f(x) = 3x - 4$.

EXAMPLE 1 *Identifying Functions*

Decide whether the relation shown in the input-output diagram is a function. If it is a function, give the domain and the range.

a. Input   Output

     1 ——→ 4
     2 ——→ 6
     3 ——→ 8
     4 ——→10

b. Input   Output

     1 ——→ 5
     2
     3 ——→ 7
     4

SOLUTION

a. The relation is not a function, because the input 3 has two outputs: 8 and 10.

b. The relation is a function. For each input there is exactly one output. The domain of the function is the set of input values 1, 2, 3, and 4. The range is the set of output values 5 and 7.

Exercises for Example 1

Decide whether the relation is a function. If it is a function, give the domain and the range.

1. Input   Output

     2 ——→ 1
     4 ——→ 3
           5
     8 ——→ 7

2. Input   Output

     1 ——→ 1
     2 ——→ 4
     3 ——→ 9
     4 ——→16

3. Input   Output

     1
     2 ——→ 4
     3 ——→ 6
     4 ——→ 8

Chapter 4

NAME _____ DATE _____

Practice with Examples

For use with pages 256–262

EXAMPLE 2 *Evaluating a Function*

Evaluate the function $f(x) = -4x + 5$ when $x = -1$.

SOLUTION

$f(x) = -4x + 5$	Write original function.
$f(-1) = -4(-1) + 5$	Substitute -1 for x.
$= 9$	Simplify.

Exercises for Example 2

Evaluate the function when $x = 3$, $x = 0$, and $x = -2$.

4. $f(x) = 9x + 2$

5. $f(x) = 0.5x + 4$

6. $f(x) = -7x + 3$

NAME _____ DATE _____

Practice with Examples

For use with pages 256–262

EXAMPLE 3 *Writing and Using a Linear Function*

While on vacation, your family traveled 1800 miles in 5 days.
Your average speed was 360 miles per day.

a. Write a linear function that models the distance that your family traveled each day.

b. Use the model to find the distance traveled after 1.5 days of travel.

SOLUTION

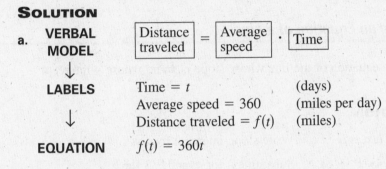

a. **VERBAL MODEL**

$$\boxed{\text{Distance traveled}} = \boxed{\text{Average speed}} \cdot \boxed{\text{Time}}$$

↓

LABELS   Time = t (days)
             Average speed = 360   (miles per day)
↓   Distance traveled = $f(t)$ (miles)

EQUATION $f(t) = 360t$

b. To find the distance traveled after 1.5 days, substitute 1.5 for t in the function.

$f(t) = 360t$ Write linear function.

$f(1.5) = 360(1.5)$ Substitute 1.5 for t.

$= 540$ Simplify.

Exercises for Example 3

7. Rework Example 3 if your family traveled 2040 miles in 6 days.

8. Rework Example 3 if your family traveled 2660 miles in 7 days.

NAME _____ DATE _____

Practice with Examples

For use with pages 273–278

GOAL **Use the slope-intercept form to write an equation of a line and model a real-life situation with a linear function**

VOCABULARY

In the **slope-intercept form** of the equation of a line, $y = mx + b$, m is the slope and b is the y-intercept.

EXAMPLE 1 *Writing an Equation of a Line*

Write an equation of the line whose slope is 4 and whose y-intercept is -3.

SOLUTION

$y = mx + b$	Write slope-intercept form.
$y = 4x + (-3)$	Substitute 4 for m and -3 for b.
$y = 4x - 3$	Simplify.

Exercises for Example 1

Write an equation of the line in slope-intercept form.

1. The slope is -2; the y-intercept is 5.

2. The slope is 1; the y-intercept is -4.

3. The slope is 0; the y-intercept is 2.

4. The slope is 3; the y-intercept is 6.

Practice with Examples

For use with pages 273–278

EXAMPLE 2 *Modeling a Real-Life Situation*

A car rental company charges a flat fee of $40 and an additional $.20 per mile to rent an automobile.

a. Write an equation to model the total charge C (in dollars) in terms of n, the number of miles driven.

b. Complete the table using the equation from part a.

Miles (n)	50	100	200	300
Total charge (C)	?	?	?	?

SOLUTION

a. **Verbal Model**

Total charge	=	Flat fee	+	Rate per mile	·	Number of miles

Labels   Total charge = C (dollars)

Flat fee = 40   (dollars)

Rate per mile = 0.20   (dollars per mile)

Number of miles = n (miles)

Algebraic Model $C = 40 + 0.20 \cdot n$ Linear model

b.

Miles (n)	50	100	200	300
Total charge (C)	50	60	80	100

Practice with Examples

For use with pages 273–278

Exercises for Example 2

5. Rework Example 2 if the company charges a flat fee of $50 and an additional $.30 per mile to rent an automobile.

6. In 1996, the enrollment in your school was approximately 1400 students. During the next three years, the enrollment increased by approximately 30 students per year.

   a. Write an equation to model the school's enrollment E in terms of t, the number of years since 1996.

   b. Use the equation to estimate the school's enrollment in the year 2002.

Practice with Examples

For use with pages 279–284

GOAL Use slope and any point on a line to write an equation of the line and use a linear model to make predictions about a real-life situation

VOCABULARY

Two nonvertical lines are **parallel** if and only if they have the same slope.

EXAMPLE 1 *Writing an Equation of a Line*

Write an equation of the line that passes through the point $(-2, 5)$ and has a slope of 3.

SOLUTION

Find the y-intercept.

$y = mx + b$	Write slope-intercept form.
$5 = 3(-2) + b$	Substitute 3 for m, -2 for x, and 5 for y.
$5 = -6 + b$	Simplify.
$11 = b$	Solve for b.

The y-intercept is $b = 11$.

Now write an equation of the line, using slope-intercept form.

$y = mx + b$	Write slope-intercept form.
$y = 3x + 11$	Substitute 3 for m and 11 for b.

Exercises for Example 1

Write an equation of the line that passes through the point and has the given slope. Write the equation in slope-intercept form.

1. $(1, -6), m = -2$

2. $(-3, -2), m = 4$

3. $(4, 5), m = -1$

Algebra 1
Practice Workbook with Examples

Chapter 5

Practice with Examples

For use with pages 279–284

EXAMPLE 2 *Writing Equations of Parallel Lines*

Write an equation of the line that is parallel to the line $y = 2x + 1$ and passes through the point $(1, 5)$.

SOLUTION

The given line has a slope of $m = 2$. A parallel line through $(1, 5)$ must also have a slope of $m = 2$. Use this information to find the y-intercept.

$$y = mx + b \qquad \text{Write slope-intercept form.}$$

$$5 = 2(1) + b \qquad \text{Substitute 2 for } m, 1 \text{ for } x, \text{ and 5 for } y.$$

$$5 = 2 + b \qquad \text{Simplify.}$$

$$3 = b \qquad \text{Solve for } b.$$

The y-intercept is $b = 3$.

Write an equation using the slope-intercept form.

$$y = mx + b \qquad \text{Write slope-intercept form.}$$

$$y = 2x + 3 \qquad \text{Substitute 2 for } m \text{ and 3 for } b.$$

Exercises for Example 2

Write an equation of the line that is parallel to the given line and passes through the given point.

4. $y = 4x - 1$, $(2, 3)$

5. $y = x + 6$, $(-3, 0)$

6. $y = -2x + 3$, $(1, -1)$

EXAMPLE 3 *Writing and Using a Linear Model*

The cost of parking in a municipal garage is a base fee plus $1.25 for each hour that you park. Your cost for 5 hours is $10.25. Write a linear equation that models the total cost y of parking in terms of the number of hours x.

SOLUTION

The slope is 1.25 and $(x, y) = (5, 10.25)$ is a point on the line.

$y = mx + b$	Write slope-intercept form.
$10.25 = (1.25)(5) + b$	Substitute 1.25 for m, 5 for x, and 10.25 for y.
$10.25 = 6.25 + b$	Simplify.
$4 = b$	The y-intercept is $b = 4$.

Write an equation of the line using $m = 1.25$ and $b = 4$.

$y = mx + b$	Write slope-intercept form.
$y = 1.25x + 4$	Substitute 1.25 for m and 4 for b.

Exercise for Example 3

7. Use the linear equation from Example 3 to estimate the total cost y of parking for 7 hours.

Practice with Examples

For use with pages 285–291

GOAL **Write an equation of a line given two points on the line and use a linear equation to model a real-life problem**

> **VOCABULARY**
>
> Two different nonvertical lines are **perpendicular** if and only if their slopes are negative reciprocals of each other.

EXAMPLE 1 *Writing an Equation Given Two Points*

Write an equation of the line that passes through the points $(1, 5)$ and $(2, 3)$.

SOLUTION

Find the slope of the line. Let $(x_1, y_1) = (1, 5)$ and $(x_2, y_2) = (2, 3)$.

$$m = \frac{y_2 - y_1}{x_2 - x_1} \qquad \text{Write formula for slope.}$$

$$= \frac{3 - 5}{2 - 1} \qquad \text{Substitute.}$$

$$= \frac{-2}{1} = -2 \qquad \text{Simplify.}$$

Find the y-intercept. Let $m = -2$, $x = 1$, and $y = 5$ and solve for b.

$y = mx + b$ Write slope-intercept form.

$5 = (-2)(1) + b$ Substitute -2 for m, 1 for x, and 5 for y.

$5 = -2 + b$ Simplify.

$7 = b$ Solve for b.

Write an equation of the line.

$y = mx + b$ Write slope-intercept form.

$y = -2x + 7$ Substitute -2 for m and 7 for b.

Algebra 1
Practice Workbook with Examples

Practice with Examples

For use with pages 285–291

Exercises for Example 1

Write an equation in slope-intercept form of the line that passes through the points.

1. $(4, 9)$ and $(1, 6)$

2. $(0, 7)$ and $(1, -1)$

3. $(-2, -3)$ and $(0, 3)$

EXAMPLE 2 ## Writing Equations of Perpendicular Lines

Write an equation of the line that is perpendicular to the line
$y = -3x + 2$ and passes through the point $(6, 5)$.

SOLUTION

The given line has a slope of $m = -3$. A perpendicular line through
$(6, 5)$ must have a slope of $m = \frac{1}{3}$. Use this information to find the
y-intercept.

$y = mx + b$	Write slope-intercept form.
$5 = \frac{1}{3}(6) + b$	Substitute $\frac{1}{3}$ for m, 6 for x, and 5 for y.
$5 = 2 + b$	Simplify.
$3 = b$	Solve for b.

The y-intercept is $b = 3$.

Write an equation using the slope-intercept form.

$y = mx + b$	Write slope-intercept form.
$y = \frac{1}{3}x + 3$	Substitute $\frac{1}{3}$ for m and 3 for b.

Practice with Examples

For use with pages 285–291

Exercises for Example 2

Write an equation of the line that is perpendicular to the given line and passes through the given point.

4. $y = 2x - 1, \ (2, 4)$

5. $y = -\frac{1}{3}x + 2, \ (5, 1)$

6. $y = -4x + 5, \ (4, 3)$

NAME _____ DATE _____

Practice with Examples

For use with pages 292–298

GOAL Find a linear equation that approximates a set of data points and determine a correlation in a set of real-life data

VOCABULARY

The line that best fits all of the data points is called the **best-fitting line**.

Positive correlation means that the points can be approximated by a line with a positive slope.

Negative correlation means that the points can be approximated by a line with a negative slope.

Points that cannot be approximated by a line have **no correlation**.

EXAMPLE 1 *Approximating a Best-Fitting Line*

Draw a scatter plot for the data. If possible, draw a best-fitting line for the scatter plot and write an equation of the line.

x	1	2	3	4	5	6
y	3	5	8	9	11	12

SOLUTION

Plot the points given by the ordered pairs (x, y). Sketch the line that appears to best fit the points.

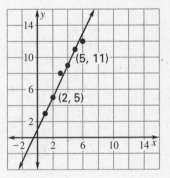

Next, find two points that lie on the best-fitting line. From the graph, choose the points $(2, 5)$ and $(5, 11)$. Calculate the slope of the line through these two points.

$$m = \frac{y_2 - y_1}{x_2 - x_1}$$ Write slope formula.

$$m = \frac{11 - 5}{5 - 2}$$ Substitute.

$$m = 2$$ Simplify.

To find the y-intercept of the line, use the values $m = 2$, $x = 2$, and $y = 5$ in the slope-intercept form.

$y = mx + b$ Write slope-intercept form.

$5 = (2)(2) + b$ Substitute 2 for m, 2 for x, and 5 for y.

$5 = 4 + b$ Simplify.

$1 = b$ Solve for b.

An equation of the best-fitting line is $y = 2x + 1$.

NAME _____ DATE _____

Practice with Examples

For use with pages 292–298

Exercises for Example 1

In Exercises 1 and 2, draw a scatter plot of the data. If possible, draw a best-fitting line for the scatter plot and write an equation of the line.

1.

x	1	2	3	4	5	6
y	7	0	1	0	7	6

2.

x	1	2	3	4	5	6
y	1	0	−2	−2	−3	−4

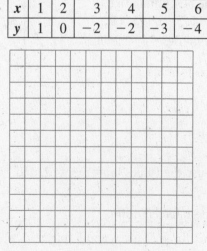

NAME _____ DATE _____

Practice with Examples

For use with pages 300–306

Exercises for Example 1

Use the point-slope form of a line to write an equation of the line that passes through the given points.

1. $(4, 5), (6, 9)$

2. $(-1, 6), (0, 3)$

3. $(-2, 8), (2, -8)$

EXAMPLE 2 *Writing and Using a Linear Model*

You are running a 10-kilometer race. At 8:00 A.M., you start the race. At 8:30 A.M., you are 4 kilometers from the finish line. Write a linear model that gives the distance d (in kilometers) from the starting line in terms of the time t (in minutes). Let t represent the number of minutes since 8:00 A.M.

SOLUTION

One point on the line is $(t_1, d_1) = (0, 10)$. Another point on the line is $(t_2, d_2) = (30, 4)$. Find the slope of the line.

$$m = \frac{\text{change in distance}}{\text{change in time}} = \frac{4 - 10}{30 - 0} = \frac{-6}{30} = -0.2$$

Use the point-slope form to write the model. Use $(0, 10)$ as (t_1, d_1).

$d - d_1 = m(t - t_1)$	Write point-slope form.
$d - 10 = -0.2(t - 0)$	Substitute for m, d_1, and t_1.
$d - 10 = -0.2t + 0$	Use distributive property.
$d = -0.2t + 10$	Add 10 to each side.

NAME _____ DATE _____

Practice with Examples

For use with pages 300–306

Exercises for Example 2

4. Use the linear model from Example 2 to predict your time to finish the race.

5. Rework Example 2 if at 8:30 A.M., you are 5 kilometers from the finish line.

Algebra 1
Practice Workbook with Examples

Practice with Examples

For use with pages 308–314

GOAL Write a linear equation in standard form and use the standard form of an equation to model real-life situations

> **VOCABULARY**
>
> The **standard form** of the equation of a line is $Ax + By = C$, where A, B, and C represent real numbers and A and B are not both zero.

EXAMPLE 1 *Writing an Equation in Standard Form*

Write $y = -\frac{3}{4}x + 5$ in standard form with integer coefficients.

SOLUTION

To write the equation in standard form, isolate the variable terms on the left and the constant term on the right.

$$y = -\tfrac{3}{4}x + 5 \qquad \text{Write original equation.}$$
$$4y = 4\left(-\tfrac{3}{4}x + 5\right) \qquad \text{Multiply each side by 4.}$$
$$4y = -3x + 20 \qquad \text{Use distributive property.}$$
$$3x + 4y = 20 \qquad \text{Add } 3x \text{ to each side.}$$

Exercises for Example 1

Write the equation in standard form with integer coefficients.

1. $y = \frac{2}{3}x - 7$

2. $y = 8 + 2x$

3. $y = 6 - \frac{1}{4}x$

Chapter 5

Practice with Examples

For use with pages 308–314

EXAMPLE 2 *Writing a Linear Equation*

Write the standard form of the equation passing through $(3, 7)$ with a slope of 2.

SOLUTION

Write the point-slope form of the equation of the line.

$$y - y_1 = m(x - x_1) \qquad \text{Write point-slope form.}$$

$$y - 7 = 2(x - 3) \qquad \text{Substitute for } y_1, m, \text{ and } x_1.$$

$$y - 7 = 2x - 6 \qquad \text{Use distributive property.}$$

$$-2x + y = 1 \qquad \text{Add } -2x \text{ and } 7 \text{ to each side.}$$

Exercises for Example 2

Write the standard form of the equation of the line that passes through the given point and has the given slope.

4. $(1, 4)$, $m = -2$

5. $(-3, 1)$, $m = 3$

6. $(5, -2)$, $m = -1$

Algebra 1
Practice Workbook with Examples

NAME _____ DATE _____

Practice with Examples

For use with pages 308–314

EXAMPLE 3 **Writing and Using a Linear Model**

You have $12 to buy peaches and blueberries for a fruit salad. Peaches cost $1.50 per pound and blueberries cost $4.00 per pound. Write a linear equation that models the different amounts of peaches x and blueberries y that you can buy.

SOLUTION

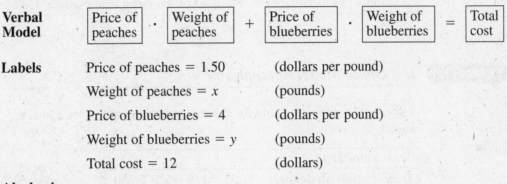

Verbal Model

| Price of peaches | · | Weight of peaches | + | Price of blueberries | · | Weight of blueberries | = | Total cost |

Labels
Price of peaches = 1.50   (dollars per pound)

Weight of peaches = x (pounds)

Price of blueberries = 4   (dollars per pound)

Weight of blueberries = y (pounds)

Total cost = 12   (dollars)

Algebraic Model $1.50x + 4y = 12$ Linear model

Exercise for Example 3

7. Copy and complete the table using the linear model in Example 3.

Peaches (lb), x	0	2	4	8
Blueberries (lb), y	?	?	?	?

NAME _____ DATE _____

Practice with Examples

For use with pages 316–322

GOAL **Determine whether a linear model is appropriate and use a linear model to make a real-life prediction**

VOCABULARY

Linear interpolation is a method of estimating the coordinates of a point that lies between two given data points.

Linear extrapolation is a method of estimating the coordinates of a point that lies to the right or left of all of the given data points.

EXAMPLE 1 *Is a Linear Model Appropriate?*

Tell whether it is reasonable for the data to be represented by a linear model.

Years since 1995	0	1	2	3
Depreciation (in dollars)	1000	740	520	250

SOLUTION

Draw a scatter plot of the data to decide whether the data can be represented by a linear model. From the scatter plot at the right, you can see that the data fall almost exactly on a line. A linear model is appropriate.

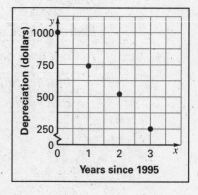

Exercises for Example 1

Tell whether it is reasonable for the graph to be represented by a linear model.

1.

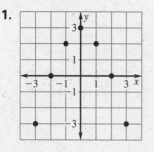

2.

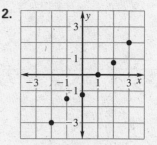

NAME _____ DATE _____

Practice with Examples

For use with pages 316–322

EXAMPLE 2 *Writing a Linear Model*

Use the scatter plot from Example 1 to write a linear model for the data.

SOLUTION

Find two points on the best-fitting line such as (0, 1000) and (3, 250).
Use these points to find the slope of the best-fitting line.

$$m = \frac{y_2 - y_1}{x_2 - x_1} = \frac{250 - 1000}{3 - 0} = \frac{-750}{3} = -250$$

Using a y-intercept of $b = 1000$ and a slope of $m = -250$, you can write
an equation of the line.

$y = mx + b$ Write slope-intercept form.

$y = -250x + 1000$ Substitute -250 for m and 1000 for b.

A linear model for the data is $y = -250x + 1000$.

Exercises for Example 2

3. Use the data given in the table.

   a. Make a scatter plot of the data.

   b. Write a linear model for the data.

Year	1990	1992	1994	1996	1998
Expenditures (in millions)	50	210	350	490	650

LESSON 5.7 CONTINUED

Chapter 5

Practice with Examples

For use with pages 316–322

EXAMPLE 3 *Linear Interpolation and Linear Extrapolation*

Use the model found in Example 2 to estimate the depreciation in 1999.

SOLUTION

You are given data for 1995–1998. Because 1999 is to the right of all of the given data, you will use linear extrapolation. You can estimate the depreciation in 1999 by substituting $x = 4$ into the linear model.

$y = -250x + 1000$ Write linear model.

$y = -250(4) + 1000$ Substitute 4 for x.

$y = -1000 + 1000 = 0$ Simplify.

The model predicts that the depreciation in the year 1999 will be $0.

Exercise for Example 3

4. Use the model found in Exercise 3 to estimate the expenditures in 1991.

NAME _____ DATE _____

Practice with Examples

For use with pages 334–339

GOAL Graph linear inequalities in one variable and solve one-step linear inequalities

---

VOCABULARY

The **graph** of a linear inequality in one variable is the set of points on a number line that represent all solutions of the inequality.

Equivalent inequalities are inequalities that have the same solution(s).

EXAMPLE 1 *Graphing a Linear Inequality*

a. Graph the inequality $3 > x$.

b. Graph the inequality $x \geq 4$.

SOLUTION

a. Use an open dot for the inequality symbol < or >.

```
       +----+----+----+----+----○----+----→
      −2   −1    0    1    2    3    4
```

b. Use a closed dot for the inequality symbol ≤ or ≥.

```
       +----+----+----+----●----+----+----→
      −4   −2    0    2    4    6    8
```

Exercises for Example 1

Graph the inequality.

1. $x \leq -1$ **2.** $x \geq 0$ **3.** $x < 0$

NAME _____ DATE _____

Practice with Examples

For use with pages 334–339

EXAMPLE 2 *Using Addition or Subtraction to Solve an Inequality*

Solve $x - 7 > -6$. Graph the solution.

SOLUTION

$x - 7 > -6$	Write original inequality.
$x - 7 + 7 > -6 + 7$	Add 7 to each side.
$x > 1$	Simplify.

The solution is all real numbers greater than 1. Check several numbers that are greater than 1 in the original inequality.

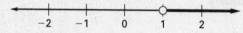

Exercises for Example 2

Solve the inequality and graph its solution.

4. $1 > y - 1$

5. $x + 3 \leq 0$

6. $k - 4 > -6$

Algebra 1
Practice Workbook with Examples

Practice with Examples

For use with pages 334–339

EXAMPLE 3 *Using Multiplication or Division to Solve an Inequality*

a. Solve $-3x \geq -12$. **b.** Solve $\dfrac{n}{-2} < 5$. **c.** Solve $4y \leq -8$.

SOLUTION

a. $-3x \geq -12$ Write original inequality.

$\dfrac{-3x}{-3} \leq \dfrac{-12}{-3}$ Divide each side by -3 and reverse inequality symbol.

$x \leq 4$ Simplify.

The solution is all real numbers less than or equal to 4. Check several numbers that are less than or equal to 4 in the original inequality.

b. $\dfrac{n}{-2} < 5$ Write original inequality.

$-2 \cdot \dfrac{n}{-2} > -2 \cdot 5$ Multiply each side by -2 and reverse inequality symbol.

$n > -10$ Simplify.

The solution is all real numbers greater than -10. Check several numbers that are greater than -10 in the original inequality.

c. $4y \leq -8$ Write original inequality.

$\dfrac{4y}{4} \leq \dfrac{-8}{4}$ Divide each side by positive 4.

$y \leq -2$ Simplify.

The solution is all real numbers less than or equal to -2. Check several numbers that are less than or equal to -2 in the original inequality.

Exercises for Example 3

Solve the inequality and graph its solution.

7. $\dfrac{x}{4} < -1$ **8.** $-2a \geq -6$ **9.** $\dfrac{t}{-2} > 3$

NAME _____ DATE _____

Practice with Examples

For use with pages 340–345

GOAL Solve multi-step linear inequalities and use linear inequalities to model and solve real-life problems

EXAMPLE 1 *Using More than One Step*

Solve $3n + 2 \leq 14$.

SOLUTION

$3n + 2 \leq 14$	Write original inequality.
$3n \leq 12$	Subtract 2 from each side.
$n \leq 4$	Divide each side by 3.

The solution is all real numbers less than or equal to 4.

Exercises for Example 1

Solve the inequality.

1. $5x - 7 > -2$

2. $9m + 2 \leq 20$

3. $13 + 4y \geq 9$

Algebra 1
Practice Workbook with Examples

NAME _____ DATE _____

Practice with Examples

For use with pages 340–345

EXAMPLE 2 *Multiplying or Dividing by a Negative Number*

Solve $11 - 2x \geq 3x + 16$.

SOLUTION

$11 - 2x \geq 3x + 16$	Write original inequality.
$-2x \geq 3x + 5$	Subtract 11 from each side.
$-5x \geq 5$	Subtract $3x$ from each side.
$x \leq -1$	Divide each side by -5 and reverse inequality.

The solution is all real numbers less than or equal to -1.

Exercises for Example 2

Solve the inequality.

4. $8 > 5 - a$

5. $-4x + 2 \leq -22$

6. $-\dfrac{y}{2} + 3 \geq 0$

NAME _____ DATE _____

Practice with Examples

EXAMPLE 3 **Writing and Using a Linear Model**

You wash dishes in a restaurant and earn $5.15 per hour. How many hours must you work to make at least $200 to buy a new snowboard?

SOLUTION

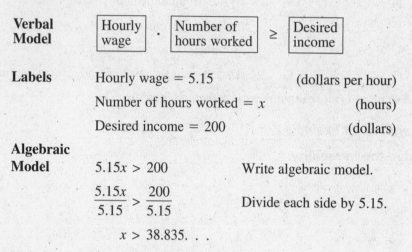

Verbal Model

| Hourly wage | · | Number of hours worked | ≥ | Desired income |

Labels   Hourly wage = 5.15   (dollars per hour)

　　　　　　Number of hours worked = x (hours)

　　　　　　Desired income = 200   (dollars)

Algebraic Model

$5.15x > 200$ Write algebraic model.

$\dfrac{5.15x}{5.15} > \dfrac{200}{5.15}$ Divide each side by 5.15.

$x > 38.835. . .$

You need to work at least 39 hours.

Exercises for Example 3

7. Rework Example 3 if you earn $4.60 per hour.

8. Rework Example 3 if you need to make $240 to buy a new snowboard.

NAME _____ DATE _____

Practice with Examples

For use with pages 346–352

GOAL Write, solve, and graph compound inequalities and model a real-life situation with a compound inequality

VOCABULARY

A **compound inequality** consists of two inequalities connected by *and* or *or*.

EXAMPLE 1 *Writing Compound Inequalities*

a. Write an inequality that represents all real numbers that are less than 0 *or* greater than 3. Graph the inequality.

b. Write an inequality that represents all real numbers that are greater than or equal to −2 *and* less than 1. Graph the inequality.

SOLUTION

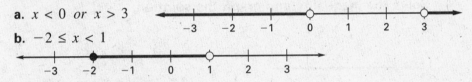

a. $x < 0$ *or* $x > 3$

b. $-2 \le x < 1$

Exercises for Example 1

Write an inequality that represents the statement and graph the inequality.

1. x is greater than −4 and less than or equal to −2

2. x is greater than 3 *or* less than −1

Algebra 1
Practice Workbook with Examples

NAME _____ DATE _____

Practice with Examples

For use with pages 346–352

EXAMPLE 2 **Solving a Compound Inequality with And**

Solve $-9 \leq -4x - 5 < 3$. Graph the solution.

SOLUTION

Isolate the variable x between the two inequality symbols.

$-9 \leq -4x - 5 < 3$	Write original inequality.
$-4 \leq -4x < 8$	Add 5 to each expression.
$1 \geq x > -2$	Divide each expression by -4 and *reverse* both inequality symbols.

The solution is all real numbers that are less than or equal to 1 *and* greater than -2.

```
    ○───┼───┼───●───┼──→
   -2  -1   0   1   2
```

Exercises for Example 2

Solve the inequality and graph the solution.

3. $-3 < 2x + 1 \leq 7$

```
←─────────────→
```

4. $-6 < -3 + x < -4$

```
←─────────────→
```

5. $2 \leq -3x + 8 < 17$

```
←─────────────→
```

NAME _____ DATE _____

Practice with Examples

For use with pages 346–352

EXAMPLE 3 *Solving a Compound Inequality with Or*

Solve $5x + 1 < -4$ *or* $6x - 2 \geq 10$. Graph the solution.

SOLUTION

You can solve each part separately.

$$5x + 1 < -4 \quad or \quad 6x - 2 \geq 10$$
$$5x < -5 \quad or \quad 6x \geq 12$$
$$x < -1 \quad or \quad x \geq 2$$

The solution is all real numbers that are less than -1 *or* greater than or equal to 2.

Exercises for Example 3

Solve the inequality and graph the solution.

6. $2x - 3 < 5$ *or* $3x + 1 \geq 16$

7. $-4x + 2 < 6$ *or* $2x \leq -6$

EXAMPLE 4 *Modeling with a Compound Inequality*

In 1985, a real estate property was sold for $145,000. The property was sold again in 1999 for $211,000. Write a compound inequality that represents the different values that the property was worth between 1985 and 1999.

SOLUTION

Use the variable v to represent the property value. Write a compound inequality with *and* to represent the different property values.

$$145,000 \leq v \leq 211,000$$

Exercise for Example 4

8. Rework Example 4 if the property was sold in 1985 for $172,000 and was sold again in 1999 for $226,000.

LESSON 6.4

Practice with Examples

For use with pages 353–358

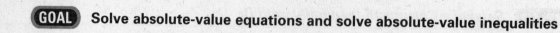

GOAL Solve absolute-value equations and solve absolute-value inequalities

EXAMPLE 1 *Solving an Absolute-Value Equation*

Solve $|4x + 2| = 18$.

SOLUTION

Because $|4x + 2| = 18$, the expression $4x + 2$ can be equal to 18 or -18.

$4x + 2$ IS POSITIVE	$4x + 2$ IS NEGATIVE
$|4x + 2| = 18$	$|4x + 2| = 18$
$4x + 2 = +18$	$4x + 2 = -18$
$4x = 16$	$4x = -20$
$x = 4$	$x = -5$

The equation has two solutions: 4 and -5.

Exercises for Example 1

Solve the equation.

1. $|x| = 8$

2. $|x - 3| = 4$

3. $|2x - 3| = 9$

NAME _____ DATE _____

Practice with Examples

For use with pages 353–358

EXAMPLE 2 *Solving an Absolute-Value Inequality*

Solve $|x + 5| \leq 1$.

SOLUTION

When an absolute value is *less than* a number, the inequalities are connected by *and*

$x + 5$ IS POSITIVE	$x + 5$ IS NEGATIVE
$|x + 5| \leq 1$	$|x + 5| \leq 1$
$x + 5 \leq +1$	$x + 5 \geq -1$ ← Reverse inequality symbol.
$x \leq -4$	$x \geq -6$

The solution is all real numbers greater than or equal to -6 *and* less than or equal to -4, which can be written as $-6 \leq x \leq -4$.

Exercises for Example 2

Solve the inequality.

4. $|x - 3| < 2$

5. $|8 + x| \leq 3$

6. $|x - 1.5| < 1$

Chapter 6

Practice with Examples

For use with pages 353–358

EXAMPLE 3 **Solving an Absolute-Value Inequality**

Solve $|2x - 1| > 5$.

SOLUTION

When an absolute value is *greater than* a number, the inequalities are connected by *or*.

$2x - 1$ IS POSITIVE	$2x - 1$ IS NEGATIVE
$|2x - 1| > 5$	$|2x - 1| > 5$
$2x - 1 > +5$	$2x - 1 < -5$ ← Reverse inequality symbol.
$2x > 6$	$2x < -4$
$x > 3$	$x < -2$

The solution of $|2x - 1| > 5$ is all real numbers greater than 3 *or* less than -2, which can be written as the compound inequality $x < -2$ *or* $x > 3$.

Exercises for Example 3

Solve the inequality.

7. $|x + 2| \geq 1$

8. $|x - 4| \geq 2$

9. $|2x + 1| > 3$

NAME _____ DATE _____

Practice with Examples

For use with pages 360–366

GOAL Graph a linear inequality in two variables and model a real-life situation using a linear inequality in two variables

---

VOCABULARY

A **linear inequality** in x and y is an inequality that can be written as $ax + by < c$, $ax + by \le c$, $ax + by > c$, or $ax + by \ge c$.

An ordered pair (x, y) is a **solution** of a linear inequality if the inequality is true when the values of x and y are substituted into the inequality.

The **graph** of a linear inequality in two variables is the graph of the solutions of the inequality.

EXAMPLE 1 *Checking Solutions of a Linear Inequality*

Check whether the ordered pair is a solution of $3x - y \ge 2$.

a. $(0, 0)$ **b.** $(2, 0)$ **c.** $(2, 3)$

SOLUTION

(x, y)	$3x - y \ge 2$	Conclusion
a. $(0, 0)$	$3(0) - 0 = 0 \not\ge 2$	$(0, 0)$ is not a solution.
b. $(2, 0)$	$3(2) - 0 = 6 \ge 2$	$(2, 0)$ is a solution.
c. $(2, 3)$	$3(2) - 3 = 3 \ge 2$	$(2, 3)$ is a solution.

Exercises for Example 1

Is each ordered pair a solution of the inequality?

1. $x + 2y < 0$; $(0, 0)$, $(-1, -2)$

2. $2x + y > 3$; $(2, 2)$, $(-2, 2)$

Practice with Examples

For use with pages 360–366

EXAMPLE 2 **Graphing a Linear Inequality in Two Variables**

Sketch the graph of $x - y < 2$.

SOLUTION

The corresponding equation is $x - y = 2$. To graph this line, first write the equation in slope-intercept form: $y = x - 2$.

Graph the line that has a slope of 1 and a y-intercept of -2. Use a dashed line to show that the points on the line are not solutions.

The origin $(0, 0)$ is a solution and it lies above the line. So, the graph of $x - y < 2$ is all points above the line $y = x - 2$.

Exercises for Example 2

Sketch the graph of the inequality.

3. $x \le 2$

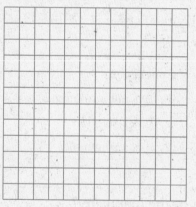

4. $y > -1$

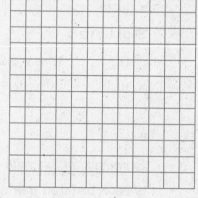

5. $y - x < 3$

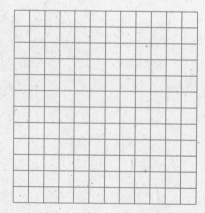

6. $2x + y \ge 4$

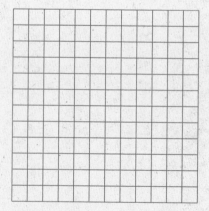

NAME _____ DATE _____

Practice with Examples

For use with pages 360–366

EXAMPLE 3 *Modeling with a Linear Inequality*

You have $16 to spend on crackers and cheese for an open house.
Crackers cost $2.50 per pound and cheese costs $4 per pound. Let x represent the number of pounds of crackers you can buy. Let y represent the
number of pounds of cheese you can buy. Write an inequality to model
the amounts of crackers and cheese you can buy.

SOLUTION

**Verbal
Model**

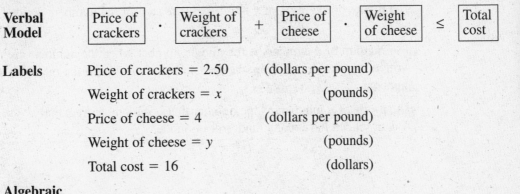

Labels   Price of crackers $= 2.50$ (dollars per pound)

Weight of crackers $= x$ (pounds)

Price of cheese $= 4$ (dollars per pound)

Weight of cheese $= y$ (pounds)

Total cost $= 16$ (dollars)

**Algebraic
Model** $2.50x + 4y \le 16$ Write algebraic model.

Exercise for Example 3

7. Graph the linear inequality in Example 3.

Chapter 6

NAME _____ DATE _____

Practice with Examples

For use with pages 368–374

GOAL **Make and use a stem-and-leaf plot to put data in order and find the mean, median, and mode of data**

VOCABULARY

A **stem-and-leaf plot** is an arrangement of digits that is used to display and order numerical data.

A **measure of central tendency** is a number that is used to represent a typical number in a data set.

The **mean,** or **average,** of *n* numbers is the sum of the numbers divided by *n*.

The **median** of *n* numbers is the middle number when the numbers are written in order. If *n* is even, the median is the average of the two middle numbers.

The **mode** of *n* numbers is the number that occurs most frequently. A data set can have many modes or no mode.

EXAMPLE 1 *Making a Stem-and-Leaf Plot*

Make an ordered stem-and-leaf plot for the data.

16   8   35   2   22   10
31   50   13   35   56   28

SOLUTION

Use the digits in the tens' place for the stem and the digits in the ones' place for the leaves. Order the leaves to make an ordered stem-and-leaf plot. The key shows you how to interpret the digits.

Ordered stem-and-leaf plot

```
        0 | 2  8
        1 | 0  3  6
        2 | 2  8
Stem    3 | 1  5  5      Leaves
        4 |
        5 | 0  6         Key: 3|1 = 31
```

Algebra 1
Practice Workbook with Examples

NAME _____ DATE _____

Practice with Examples

For use with pages 368–374

Chapter 6

Exercises for Example 1

1. Use the stem-and-leaf plot from Example 1 to list the data in increasing order.

2. Make an ordered stem-and-leaf plot for the data and use the result to list the data in increasing order.

   16   7   38   19   11   26   2   33   27   39   2

EXAMPLE 2 **Finding the Mean, Median, and Mode**

Find the measure of central tendency of the data given in Example 1.

a. mean   **b.** median   **c.** mode

SOLUTION

a. To find the mean, add the 12 numbers and divide by 12.

$$\text{mean} = \frac{2 + 8 + 10 + 13 + 16 + 22 + 28 + 31 + 35 + 35 + 50 + 56}{12}$$

$$= \frac{306}{12}$$

The mean is 25.5.

b. To find the median, write the numbers in order and find the middle number. To order the numbers, use the ordered stem-and-leaf plot from Example 1.

   2   8   10   13   16   22   28   31   35   35   50   56

Because $n = 12$ is even, the median is the average of the two middle numbers. The median is

$$\frac{22 + 28}{2} = 25.$$

c. To find the mode, use the ordered list in part (b). The mode is 35.

NAME _____ DATE _____

Practice with Examples

For use with pages 368–374

Exercise for Example 2

3. Find the mean, median, and mode of the data in Exercise 2.

Algebra 1
Practice Workbook with Examples

Practice with Examples

For use with pages 375–381

GOAL Draw a box-and-whisker plot to organize real-life data and read and interpret a box-and-whisker plot of real-life data

---

VOCABULARY

A **box-and-whisker plot** is a data display that divides a set of data into four parts.

The median or **second quartile** separates the set into two halves: the numbers that are below the median and the numbers that are above the median.

The **first quartile** is the median of the lower half.

The **third quartile** is the median of the upper half.

EXAMPLE 1 *Organizing Data*

The 1998 average monthly temperatures for your town are given below as ordered data.

33   35   40   42   47   52   54   57   64   66   67   72

a. Use the ordered data to find the quartiles.

b. Draw a box-and-whisker plot of the data.

SOLUTION

a. Second quartile: $\dfrac{52 + 54}{2} = 53$

First quartile: $\dfrac{40 + 42}{2} = 41$

Third quartile: $\dfrac{64 + 66}{2} = 65$

Practice with Examples

For use with pages 375–381

b. Draw a number line that includes the least number 33 and the greatest number 72 in the data set. Plot the least number, the quartiles, and the greatest number. Draw a line from the least number to the greatest number below your number line. Plot the same points on that line.

The "box" extends from the first to the third quartile. Draw a vertical line in the box at the second quartile. The "whiskers" connect the box to the least and greatest numbers.

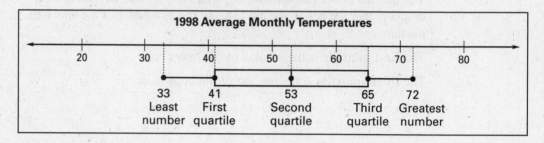

1998 Average Monthly Temperatures

Exercise for Example 1

1. Draw a box-and-whisker plot of the ordered data.

1   7   9   12   14   22   24   25

NAME _____ DATE _____

Practice with Examples

For use with pages 375–381

EXAMPLE 2 *Interpreting a Box-and-Whisker Plot*

The box-and-whisker plot below shows the number (in millions) of
personal computers in the United States from 1985 to 1995.

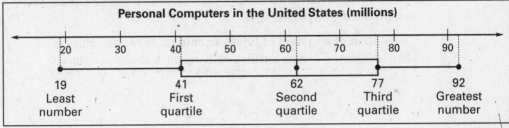

Personal Computers in the United States (millions)

| 20 | 30 | 40 | 50 | 60 | 70 | 80 | 90 |

| 19 | | 41 | | 62 | | 77 | | 92 |
| Least number | | First quartile | | Second quartile | | Third quartile | | Greatest number |

a. What is the median number of personal computers in the United
States from 1985 to 1995?

b. What is the least number of personal computers in the United States
from 1985 to 1995?

SOLUTION

a. The median number of personal computers in the United States from
1985 to 1995 is about 62 million.

b. The least number of personal computers in the United States from
1985 to 1995 is about 19 million.

Exercise for Example 2

2. What is the greatest number of personal computers in the United
States from 1985 to 1995?

Practice with Examples

For use with pages 398–403

GOAL Solve a system of linear equations by graphing and model a real-life problem using a linear system

VOCABULARY

Two equations in two variables form a **system of linear equations** or simply a **linear system.**

A **solution of a system of linear equations** in two variables is an ordered pair (x, y) that satisfies each equation in the system.

EXAMPLE 1 *Using the Graph-and-Check Method*

Solve the linear system graphically. Check the solution algebraically.

$$-3x + y = -7 \qquad \text{Equation 1}$$
$$2x + 2y = 10 \qquad \text{Equation 2}$$

SOLUTION

Write each equation in slope-intercept form.

$$y = 3x - 7 \qquad \text{Slope: 3, } y\text{-intercept: } -7$$
$$y = -x + 5 \qquad \text{Slope: } -1, y\text{-intercept: 5}$$

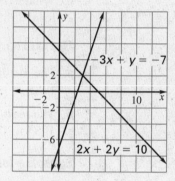

Graph each equation. The lines appear to intersect at $(3, 2)$.

To check $(3, 2)$ as a solution algebraically, substitute 3 for x and 2 for y in each original equation.

EQUATION 1   EQUATION 2

$$-3x + y = -7 \qquad 2x + 2y = 10$$
$$-3(3) + 2 \overset{?}{=} -7 \qquad 2(3) + 2(2) \overset{?}{=} 10$$
$$-7 = -7 \qquad\qquad 10 = 10$$

Because $(3, 2)$ is a solution of each equation in the linear system, it is a solution of the linear system.

Algebra 1
Practice Workbook with Examples

Chapter 7

NAME _____ DATE _____

Practice with Examples

For use with pages 398–403

Exercises for Example 1

Graph and check to solve each linear system.

1. $y = -x + 5$

$\quad y = x + 1$

2. $2x - y = 2$

$\quad x = 4$

3. $2x + y = 2$

$\quad x - y = 4$

EXAMPLE 2 ## Using a Linear System to Model a Real-Life Problem

Tickets for the theater are $5 for the balcony and $10 for the orchestra.
If 600 tickets were sold and the total receipts were $4750, how many
tickets were sold for the orchestra?

SOLUTION

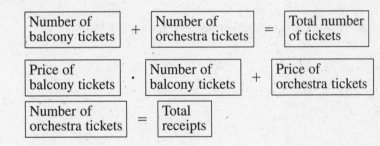

Verbal Model

| Number of balcony tickets | + | Number of orchestra tickets | = | Total number of tickets |

| Price of balcony tickets | · | Number of balcony tickets | + | Price of orchestra tickets | · |

| Number of orchestra tickets | = | Total receipts |

Chapter 7

LESSON
7.1
CONTINUED

NAME _____ DATE _____

Practice with Examples

For use with pages 398–403

Labels	Price of balcony tickets = 5	(dollars)
	Number of balcony tickets = x	(tickets)
	Price of orchestra tickets = 10	(dollars)
	Number of orchestra tickets = y	(tickets)
	Total number of tickets = 600	(tickets)
	Total receipts = 4750	(dollars)

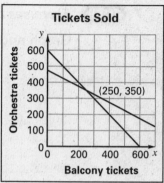

Algebraic $x + y = 600$ Equation 1 (tickets)
Model $5x + 10y = 4750$ Equation 2 (receipts)

Graph the system. Check the solution:
$250 + 350 = 600$ and $5(250) + 10(350) = 1250 + 3500 = 4750$.

350 orchestra tickets were sold.

Exercises for Example 2

4. Algebraically check the solution for Example 2.

5. Rework Example 2 if 800 tickets were sold.

6. Rework Example 2 if total receipts were $3500.

Chapter 7

Practice with Examples

For use with pages 405–410

GOAL Use substitution to solve a linear system and model a real-life situation using a linear system

EXAMPLE 1 *The Substitution Method*

Solve the linear system. $x + y = 1$ Equation 1

$2x - 3y = 12$ Equation 2

SOLUTION

Solve for y in Equation 1.

$y = -x + 1$ Revised Equation 1

Substitute $-x + 1$ for y in Equation 2 and solve for x.

$2x - 3y = 12$	Write Equation 2.
$2x - 3(-x + 1) = 12$	Substitute $-x + 1$ for y.
$2x + 3x - 3 = 12$	Distribute the -3.
$5x - 3 = 12$	Simplify.
$5x = 15$	Add 3 to each side.
$x = 3$	Solve for x.

To find the value of y, substitute 3 for x in the revised Equation 1.

$y = -x + 1$	Write revised Equation 1.
$y = -3 + 1$	Substitute 3 for x.
$y = -2$	Solve for y.

The solution is $(3, -2)$.

Exercises for Example 1

Use the substitution method to solve the linear system.

1. $x + 2y = -5$ **2.** $3x - 2y = 4$ **3.** $3x + y = -2$

$4x - 3y = 2$ $x + 3y = 5$ $x + 3y = 2$

Practice with Examples

For use with pages 405–410

EXAMPLE 2 ## *Writing and Using a Linear System*

An investor bought 225 shares of stock, stock A at $50 per share and stock B at $75 per share. If $13,750 worth of stock was purchased, how many shares of each kind did the investor buy?

SOLUTION

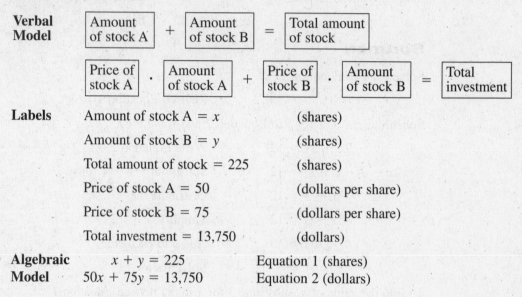

Verbal Model

| Amount of stock A | + | Amount of stock B | = | Total amount of stock |

| Price of stock A | · | Amount of stock A | + | Price of stock B | · | Amount of stock B | = | Total investment |

Labels

Amount of stock A = x (shares)

Amount of stock B = y (shares)

Total amount of stock = 225   (shares)

Price of stock A = 50   (dollars per share)

Price of stock B = 75   (dollars per share)

Total investment = 13,750   (dollars)

Algebraic Model

$x + y = 225$ Equation 1 (shares)

$50x + 75y = 13,750$ Equation 2 (dollars)

Practice with Examples

For use with pages 405–410

Solve for y in Equation 1.

$y = -x + 225$ Revised Equation 1

Substitute $-x + 225$ for y in Equation 2 and solve for x.

$50x + 75y = 13{,}750$	Write Equation 2.
$50x + 75(-x + 225) = 13{,}750$	Substitute $-x + 225$ for y.
$50x - 75x + 16{,}875 = 13{,}750$	Distribute the 75.
$-25x = -3125$	Simplify.
$x = 125$	Solve for x.

To find the value of y, substitute 125 for x in the revised Equation 1.

$y = -x + 225$	Write revised Equation 1.
$y = -125 + 225$	Substitute 125 for x.
$y = 100$	Solve for y.

The solution is (125, 100).

Exercises for Example 2

4. Rework Example 2 if the investor bought 200 shares of stock.

5. Rework Example 2 if $16,250 worth of stock was purchased.

Practice with Examples

For use with pages 411–417

 GOAL Use linear combinations to solve a system of linear equations and model a real-life problem using a system of linear equations

---

VOCABULARY

A **linear combination** of two equations is an equation obtained by adding one of the equations (or a multiple of one of the equations) to the other equation.

EXAMPLE 1   *Using Multiplication First*

Solve the linear system. $4x - 3y = 11$ Equation 1
$3x + 2y = -13$ Equation 2

SOLUTION

The equations are arranged with like terms in columns. You can get the coefficients of y to be opposites by multiplying the first equation by 2 and the second equation by 3.

$4x - 3y = 11$ Multiply by 2. $8x - 6y = 22$

$3x + 2y = -13$ Multiply by 3. $\underline{9x + 6y = -39}$

$17x = -17$ Add the equations.

$x = -1$ Solve for x.

Substitute -1 for x in the second equation and solve for y.

$3x + 2y = -13$ Write Equation 2.

$3(-1) + 2y = -13$ Substitute -1 for x.

$-3 + 2y = -13$ Simplify.

$y = -5$ Solve for y.

The solution is $(-1, -5)$.

NAME _____ DATE _____

Practice with Examples

For use with pages 411–417

Exercises for Example 1

Use linear combinations to solve the system of linear equations.

1. $x + 2y = 5$
$3x - 2y = 7$

2. $x + y = 1$
$2x - 3y = 12$

3. $x - y = -4$
$x + 2y = 5$

EXAMPLE 2 ## *Writing and Using a Linear System*

A pharmacy mailed 300 advertisements, smaller ads requiring $.33 postage and larger ads requiring $.55 postage. If the total cost of postage was $121, find the number of advertisements mailed at each rate.

SOLUTION

Verbal Model				

$$\boxed{\text{Number of smaller ads}} + \boxed{\text{Number of larger ads}} = \boxed{\text{Total number of ads}}$$

$$\boxed{\text{Postage for smaller ads}} \cdot \boxed{\text{Number of smaller ads}} + \boxed{\text{Postage for larger ads}} \cdot \boxed{\text{Number of larger ads}} =$$

$$\boxed{\text{Total cost of postage}}$$

Labels
Number of smaller ads $= x$ (ads)

Number of larger ads $= y$ (ads)

Total number of ads $= 300$ (ads)

Postage for smaller ads $= 0.33$ (dollars per ad)

Postage for larger ads $= 0.55$ (dollars per ad)

Total cost of postage $= 121$ (dollars)

Algebraic Model
$x + y = 300$ Equation 1 (ads)
$0.33x + 0.55y = 121$ Equation 2 (dollars)

NAME _____ DATE _____

Practice with Examples

For use with pages 411–417

Use linear combinations to solve for y.

$-0.33x - 0.33y = -99$ Multiply Equation 1 by -0.33.

$\underline{0.33x + 0.55y = 121}$ Write Equation 2.

$0.22y = 22$ Add the equations.

$y = 100$ Solve for y.

Substitute 100 for y in Equation 1 and solve for x.

$x + y = 300$ Write Equation 1.

$x + 100 = 300$ Substitute 100 for y.

$x = 200$ Solve for x.

The solution is (200, 100). The pharmacy mailed 200 smaller ads and 100 larger ads.

Exercises for Example 2

4. Rework Example 2 if the total cost of postage was $154.

5. Rework Example 2 if the pharmacy mailed 320 advertisements.

NAME _____ DATE _____

Practice with Examples

For use with pages 418–424

GOAL Choose the best method to solve a linear system and use a system to model real-life problems

EXAMPLE 1 *Choosing a Solution Method*

Your cousin borrowed $6000, some on a home-equity loan at an interest rate of 9.5% and the rest on a consumer loan at an interest rate of 11%. Her total interest paid was $645. How much did she borrow at each rate?

SOLUTION

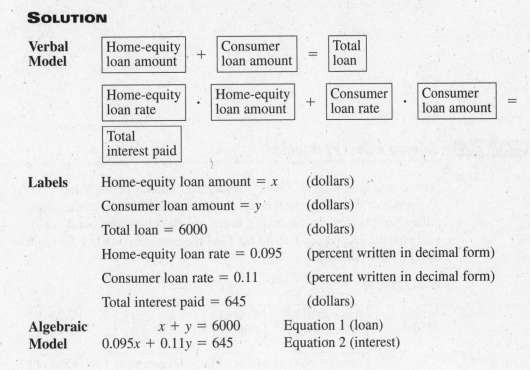

| **Verbal Model** | Home-equity loan amount | + | Consumer loan amount | = | Total loan |

Home-equity loan rate · Home-equity loan amount + Consumer loan rate · Consumer loan amount = Total interest paid

Labels	Home-equity loan amount $= x$	(dollars)
	Consumer loan amount $= y$	(dollars)
	Total loan $= 6000$	(dollars)
	Home-equity loan rate $= 0.095$	(percent written in decimal form)
	Consumer loan rate $= 0.11$	(percent written in decimal form)
	Total interest paid $= 645$	(dollars)

| **Algebraic Model** | $x + y = 6000$ | Equation 1 (loan) |
| | $0.095x + 0.11y = 645$ | Equation 2 (interest) |

Chapter 7

Practice with Examples

For use with pages 418–424

Because the coefficients of x and y are 1 in Equation 1, use the substitution method. You can solve Equation 1 for x and substitute the result into Equation 2. You will obtain 5000 for y. Substitute 5000 into Equation 1 and solve for x. You will obtain 1000 for x.

The solution is $1000 borrowed at 9.5% and $5000 borrowed at 11%.

Exercise for Example 1

1. Choose a method to solve the linear system. Explain your choice.

   a. $2x - y = 3$
   $x + 3y = 5$

   b. $4x + 4y = 16$
   $-2x + 5y = 9$

   c. $x - 3y = 3$
   $5x + 2y = 14$

EXAMPLE 2 *Solving a Cost Problem*

For a community bake sale, you purchased 12 pounds of sugar and 15 pounds of flour. Your total cost was $9.30. The next day, at the same prices, you purchased 4 pounds of sugar and 10 pounds of flour. Your total cost the second day was $4.60. Find the cost per pound of the sugar and the flour purchases.

SOLUTION

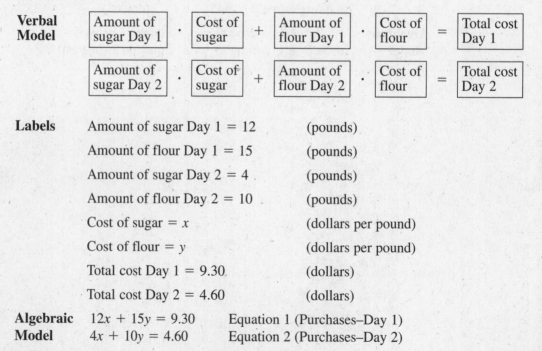

Verbal Model

$$\boxed{\text{Amount of sugar Day 1}} \cdot \boxed{\text{Cost of sugar}} + \boxed{\text{Amount of flour Day 1}} \cdot \boxed{\text{Cost of flour}} = \boxed{\text{Total cost Day 1}}$$

$$\boxed{\text{Amount of sugar Day 2}} \cdot \boxed{\text{Cost of sugar}} + \boxed{\text{Amount of flour Day 2}} \cdot \boxed{\text{Cost of flour}} = \boxed{\text{Total cost Day 2}}$$

Labels

Amount of sugar Day 1 = 12	(pounds)
Amount of flour Day 1 = 15	(pounds)
Amount of sugar Day 2 = 4	(pounds)
Amount of flour Day 2 = 10	(pounds)
Cost of sugar = x	(dollars per pound)
Cost of flour = y	(dollars per pound)
Total cost Day 1 = 9.30	(dollars)
Total cost Day 2 = 4.60	(dollars)

Algebraic Model

$12x + 15y = 9.30$ Equation 1 (Purchases–Day 1)

$4x + 10y = 4.60$ Equation 2 (Purchases–Day 2)

Chapter 7

NAME _____ DATE _____

Practice with Examples

For use with pages 418–424

Use linear combinations to solve this linear system because none of the variables has a coefficient of 1 or −1. You can get the coefficients of x to be opposites by multiplying Equation 2 by −3. You will obtain 0.30 for y. Substitute 0.30 for y into Equation 1 and solve for x. You will obtain 0.40 for x.

The solution of the linear system is (0.40, 0.30). You conclude that sugar costs $.40 per pound and flour costs $.30 per pound.

Exercise for Example 2

2. Rework Example 2 if the cost of the first purchase was $7.95 and the cost of the second purchase was $3.90.

NAME _____ DATE _____

Practice with Examples

For use with pages 426–431

GOAL Identify linear systems as having one solution, no solution, or infinitely many solutions and model real-life problems using a linear system

EXAMPLE 1 *A Linear System with No Solution*

Show that the linear system has no solution.

$3x - y = 1$ Equation 1

$3x - y = -2$ Equation 2

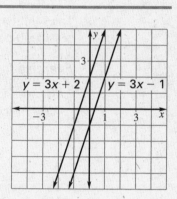

SOLUTION

Method 1:   GRAPHING Rewrite each equation in slope-intercept form. Then graph the linear system.

$y = 3x - 1$ Revised Equation 1

$y = 3x + 2$ Revised Equation 2

Because the lines have the same slope but different y-intercepts, they are parallel. Parallel lines never intersect, so the system has no solution.

Method 2:   SUBSTITUTION Because Equation 2 can be revised to $y = 3x + 2$, you can substitute $3x + 2$ for y in Equation 1.

$3x - y = 1$ Write Equation 1.

$3x - (3x + 2) = 1$ Substitute $3x + 2$ for y.

$-2 = 1$ Simplify. False statement.

The variables are eliminated and you have a statement that is not true regardless of the values of x and y. The system has no solution.

Exercises for Example 1

Choose a method to solve the linear system and tell how many solutions the system has.

1. $2x - y = 1$

     $6x - 3y = 12$

2. $x + y = 5$

     $3x + 3y = 7$

3. $2x + 6y = 6$

     $x + 3y = -3$

Algebra 1
Practice Workbook with Examples

NAME _____ DATE _____

Practice with Examples

For use with pages 426–431

EXAMPLE 2 *A Linear System with Many Solutions*

Use linear combinations to show that the linear system has infinitely many solutions.

$$3x + y = 4 \qquad \text{Equation 1}$$
$$6x + 2y = 8 \qquad \text{Equation 2}$$

SOLUTION

You can multiply Equation 1 by -2.

$$-6x - 2y = -8 \qquad \text{Multiply Equation 1 by } -2.$$
$$\underline{6x + 2y = 8} \qquad \text{Write Equation 2.}$$
$$0 = 0 \qquad \text{Add the equations.}$$

The variables are eliminated and you have a statement that is true regardless of the values of x and y. The system has infinitely many solutions.

Exercises for Example 2

Choose a method to solve the linear system and tell how many solutions the system has.

4. $2x + 3y = 6$
    $6x + 9y = 18$

5. $4x + 6y = 12$
    $6x + 9y = 18$

6. $4x - 2y = 6$
    $2x - y = 3$

Chapter 7

NAME _____ DATE _____

Practice with Examples

For use with pages 426–431

EXAMPLE 3 *Modeling a Real-Life Problem*

An artist is buying art supplies. She buys 4 sketchpads and 2 palettes. She pays $16 for the supplies. The following week, at the same prices, she buys 2 sketchpads and one palette and pays $8. Can you find the price of one sketchpad? Explain.

SOLUTION

Let x represent the price of a sketchpad and let y represent the price of a palette. Determine the number of solutions of the linear system:

$$4x + 2y = 16 \qquad \text{Equation 1}$$
$$2x + y = 8 \qquad \text{Equation 2}$$

Use the graphing method to identify the number of solutions for the linear system. Rewrite each equation in slope-intercept form and graph the linear system.

$$y = -2x + 8 \qquad \text{Revised Equation 1}$$
$$y = -2x + 8 \qquad \text{Revised Equation 2}$$

The equations represent the same line. Any point on the line is a solution. You cannot find the price of one sketchpad.

Exercise for Example 3

7. Rework Example 3, if the cost of the second purchase was $5 for one sketchpad and one palette.

Chapter 7

NAME _____ DATE _____

Practice with Examples

For use with pages 432–438

GOAL Solve a system of linear inequalities by graphing and use a system of linear inequalities to model a real-life situation

---

VOCABULARY

Two or more linear inequalities form a **system of linear inequalities** or simply a **system of inequalities.**

A **solution** of a system of linear inequalities is an ordered pair that is a solution of each inequality in the system.

The **graph** of a system of linear inequalities is the graph of all solutions of the system.

EXAMPLE 1 ## *A Triangular or Quadrilateral Solution Region*

Graph the system of linear inequalities.

$x - y \geq 0$	Inequality 1
$x + y \geq 0$	Inequality 2
$x \leq 3$	Inequality 3
$y \leq 2$	Inequality 4

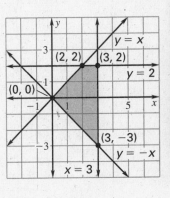

SOLUTION

Graph all four inequalities in the same coordinate system. The graph of the system is the overlap, or intersection, of the four half-planes shown.

When graphing a system of linear inequalities, find each corner point (or vertex). The graph of the system for Example 1 has four corner points: $(0, 0)$, $(2, 2)$, $(3, 2)$, and $(3, -3)$.

Chapter 7

NAME _____ DATE _____

Practice with Examples

For use with pages 432–438

Exercises for Example 1

Graph the system of linear inequalities.

1. $x + y \leq 5$

   $x > 1$

   $y > -1$

2. $2x + 3y < 6$

   $2x + y \leq 2$

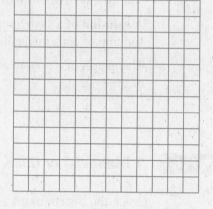

3. $y \geq x - 1$

   $y \leq -x + 1$

   $y \geq -1$

   $x \geq -1$

Algebra 1
Practice Workbook with Examples

NAME _____ DATE _____

Practice with Examples

For use with pages 432–438

EXAMPLE 2 **Writing a System of Linear Inequalities**

Suppose that you can spend no more than $72 for compact discs and
videos. Discs cost $18 each and videos cost $9 each. Write a system of
linear inequalities that shows the various numbers of discs and videos
that you can buy.

SOLUTION

**Verbal
Model**
$$\boxed{\text{Number of discs}} \geq 0$$

$$\boxed{\text{Number of videos}} \geq 0$$

$$\boxed{\begin{array}{c}\text{Number}\\\text{of discs}\end{array}} \cdot \boxed{\begin{array}{c}\text{Cost of}\\\text{a disc}\end{array}} + \boxed{\begin{array}{c}\text{Number}\\\text{of videos}\end{array}} \cdot \boxed{\begin{array}{c}\text{Cost of}\\\text{a video}\end{array}} \leq 72$$

Labels   Number of discs $= x$ (no units)

Number of videos $= y$ (no units)

Cost of a disc $= 18$ (dollars)

Cost of a video $= 9$ (dollars)

Algebraic $x \geq 0$ Inequality 1
Model $y \geq 0$ Inequality 2
          $18x + 9y \leq 72$ Inequality 3

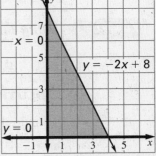

The graph of the system of inequalities is shown. Any
point in the shaded region is a solution of the system.
Because you cannot buy a fraction of a disc or video, only
ordered pairs of integers in the shaded region will answer the problem.

Exercises for Example 2

4. Rework Example 3 if you can spend no more than $90.

5. Rework Example 3 if discs cost $16 each and videos cost $8 each.

Algebra 1
Practice Workbook with Examples

NAME _____ DATE _____

Practice with Examples

For use with pages 450–455

GOAL Use properties of exponents to multiply exponential expressions and use powers to model real-life problems

---

VOCABULARY

Let a and b be numbers and let m and n be positive integers.

Product of Powers Property
To multiply powers having the same base, add the exponents.
$a^m \cdot a^n = a^{m+n}$ 　　　Example: $3^2 \cdot 3^7 = 3^{2+7} = 3^9$

Power of a Power Property
To find a power of a power, multiply the exponents.
$(a^m)^n = a^{m \cdot n}$ 　　　Example: $(5^2)^4 = 5^{2 \cdot 4} = 5^8$

Power of a Product Property
To find a power of a product, find the power of each factor and multiply.
$(a \cdot b)^m = a^m \cdot b^m$ 　　　Example: $(2 \cdot 3)^6 = 2^6 \cdot 3^6$

EXAMPLE 1 *Using the Product of Powers Property*

　a. $4^3 \cdot 4^5$ 　　　　　　　　　**b.** $(-x)(-x)^2$

SOLUTION

To multiply powers having the same base, add the exponents.

a. $4^3 \cdot 4^5 = 4^{3+5}$ 　　　　　　**b.** $(-x)(-x)^2 = (-x)^1(-x)^2$
　　　　　$= 4^8$ 　　　　　　　　　　　　　　　$= (-x)^{1+2}$
　　　　　　　　　　　　　　　　　　　　　　　$= (-x)^3$

Exercises for Example 1

Use the product of powers property to simplify the expression.

1. $m \cdot m$ 　　　　　　　　　　**2.** $6^2 \cdot 6^3$

3. $y^4 \cdot y^3$ 　　　　　　　　　　**4.** $3 \cdot 3^5$

NAME _____ DATE _____

Practice with Examples

For use with pages 450–455

EXAMPLE 2 *Using the Power of a Power Property*

a. $(z^4)^5$ **b.** $(2^3)^2$

SOLUTION

To find a power of a power, multiply the exponents.

a. $(z^4)^5 = z^{4 \cdot 5}$ **b.** $(2^3)^2 = 2^{3 \cdot 2}$

           $= z^{20}$ $= 2^6$

Exercises for Example 2

Use the power of a power property to simplify the expression.

5. $(w^7)^3$ **6.** $(7^3)^5$

7. $(t^2)^6$ **8.** $[(-2)^3]^2$

EXAMPLE 3 *Using the Power of a Product Property*

Simplify $(-4mn)^2$.

SOLUTION

To find a power of a product, find the power of each factor and multiply.

$$
\begin{aligned}
(-4mn)^2 &= (-4 \cdot m \cdot n)^2 &&\text{Identify factors.} \\
&= (-4)^2 \cdot m^2 \cdot n^2 &&\text{Raise each factor to a power.} \\
&= 16m^2n^2 &&\text{Simplify.}
\end{aligned}
$$

Algebra 1
Practice Workbook with Examples

Chapter 8

Practice with Examples

For use with pages 450–455

Exercises for Example 3

Use the power of a product property to simplify the expression.

9. $(5x)^3$

10. $(10s)^2$

11. $(-x)^4$

12. $(-3y)^3$

EXAMPLE 4 *Using Powers to Model Real-Life Problems*

You are planting two square vegetable gardens. The side of the larger garden is twice as long as the side of the smaller garden. Find the ratio of the area of the larger garden to the area of the smaller garden.

SOLUTION

$$\text{Ratio} = \frac{(2x)^2}{x^2} = \frac{2^2 \cdot x^2}{x^2} = \frac{4x^2}{x^2} = \frac{4}{1}$$

Exercise for Example 4

13. Rework Example 4 if the side of the larger garden is three times as long as the side of the smaller garden.

Chapter 8

GOAL **Evaluate powers that have zero and negative exponents and graph exponential functions**

> ### VOCABULARY
>
> Let a be a nonzero number and let n be a positive integer.
> - A nonzero number to the zero power is 1: $a^0 = 1$, $a \neq 0$.
> - a^{-n} is the reciprocal of a^n: $a^{-n} = \dfrac{1}{a^n}$, $a \neq 0$.
>
> An **exponential function** is a function of the form $y = ab^x$, where y is the amount after x periods, a is the initial value, and b is the growth factor.

EXAMPLE 1 ### *Powers with Zero and Negative Exponents*

Evaluate the exponential expression. Write your answer as a fraction in simplest form.

a. $(-8)^0$ b. 4^{-2}

SOLUTION

a. $(-8)^0 = 1$ A nonzero number to the zero power is 1.

b. $4^{-2} = \dfrac{1}{4^2} = \dfrac{1}{16}$ 4^{-2} is the reciprocal of 4^2.

Exercises for Example 1

Evaluate the exponential expression. Write your answer as a fraction in simplest form.

1. 73^0

2. $\left(\frac{1}{2}\right)^{-1}$

3. 13^{-x}

NAME _____ DATE _____

Practice with Examples

For use with pages 456–461

EXAMPLE 2 *Simplifying Exponential Expressions*

Rewrite the expression with positive exponents.

a. $5y^{-1}z^{-2}$ b. $(2x)^{-3}$

SOLUTION

a. $5y^{-1}z^{-2} = 5 \cdot \dfrac{1}{y} \cdot \dfrac{1}{z^2} = \dfrac{5}{yz^2}$

b. $(2x)^{-3} = 2^{-3} \cdot x^{-3}$ Use power of a product property.

$\quad = \dfrac{1}{2^3} \cdot \dfrac{1}{x^3}$ Write reciprocals of 2^3 and x^3.

$\quad = \dfrac{1}{8x^3}$ Multiply fractions.

Exercises for Example 2

Rewrite the expression with positive exponents.

4. $(13y)^{-1}$ 5. $\dfrac{1}{(2x)^{-4}}$ 6. $(2c)^{-4}d$

EXAMPLE 3 *Evaluating Exponential Expressions*

Evaluate the expression.

$(3^{-2})^{-3}$

SOLUTION

$(3^{-2})^{-3} = 3^{-2 \cdot (-3)}$ Use power of a power property.

$\quad = 3^6$ Multiply exponents.

$\quad = 729$ Evaluate.

Exercises for Example 3

Evaluate the expression.

7. $8^{-1} \cdot 8^1$ 8. $4^6 \cdot 4^{-4}$ 9. $(5^{-2})^2$

NAME ______________________ DATE __________

Practice with Examples

For use with pages 456–461

EXAMPLE 4 Graphing an Exponential Function

Sketch the graph of $y = 3^x$.

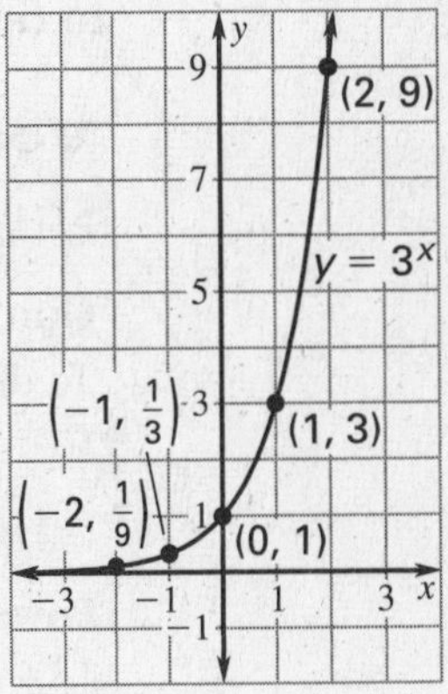

SOLUTION

Make a table that includes negative *x*-values.

x	-2	-1	0	1	2
3^x	$3^{-2} = \frac{1}{9}$	$3^{-1} = \frac{1}{3}$	$3^0 = 1$	3	9

Draw a coordinate plane and plot the five points given by the table. Draw a smooth curve through the points.

Exercise for Example 4

10. Sketch the graph of $y = 4^x$.

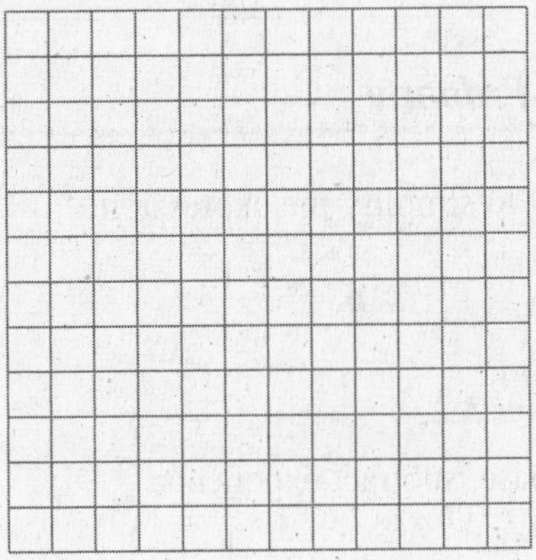

Practice with Examples

For use with pages 463–469

GOAL Use the division properties of exponents to evaluate powers and simplify expressions, and use the division properties of exponents to find a probability

---

VOCABULARY

Let a and b be numbers and let m and n be integers.

Quotient of Powers Property

To divide powers having the same base, subtract exponents.

$$\frac{a^m}{a^n} = a^{m-n}, \; a \neq 0 \qquad \text{Example: } \frac{3^7}{3^5} = 3^{7-5} = 3^2$$

Power of a Quotient Property

To find a power of a quotient, find the power of the numerator and the power of the denominator and divide.

$$\left(\frac{a}{b}\right)^m = \frac{a^m}{b^m}, \; b \neq 0 \qquad \text{Example: } \left(\frac{4}{5}\right)^3 = \frac{4^3}{5^3}$$

EXAMPLE 1 *Using the Quotient of Powers Property*

Use the quotient of powers property to simplify the expression.

a. $\dfrac{8^2 \cdot 8^4}{8^3}$

b. $z^7 \cdot \dfrac{1}{z^8}$

SOLUTION

To divide powers having the same base, subtract exponents.

a.
$$\frac{8^2 \cdot 8^4}{8^3} = \frac{8^6}{8^3}$$
$$= 8^{6-3}$$
$$= 8^3$$

b.
$$z^7 \cdot \frac{1}{z^8} = \frac{z^7}{z^8}$$
$$= z^{7-8}$$
$$= z^{-1}$$
$$= \frac{1}{z}$$

Exercises for Example 1

Use the quotient of powers property to simplify the expression.

1. $\dfrac{10^4}{10}$

2. $\dfrac{3^2}{3^3}$

3. $\dfrac{1}{y^2} \cdot y^8$

NAME _____ DATE _____

Practice with Examples

For use with pages 463–469

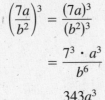 **EXAMPLE 2** *Simplifying an Expression*

Simplify the expression. $\left(\dfrac{7a}{b^2}\right)^3$

SOLUTION

$$\left(\dfrac{7a}{b^2}\right)^3 = \dfrac{(7a)^3}{(b^2)^3} \qquad \text{Power of a quotient}$$

$$= \dfrac{7^3 \cdot a^3}{b^6} \qquad \text{Power of a product and power of a power}$$

$$= \dfrac{343a^3}{b^6} \qquad \text{Simplify.}$$

Exercises for Example 2

Simplify the expression. The simplified expression should have no negative exponents.

4. $\left(\dfrac{2}{x^3}\right)^4$

5. $\dfrac{z \cdot z^5}{z^2}$

6. $\left(\dfrac{5y^2}{w}\right)^2$

Chapter 8

NAME _____ DATE _____

Practice with Examples

For use with pages 463–469

EXAMPLE 3 ***Using the Power of a Quotient Property***

You toss a fair coin four times. Show that the probability of getting four tails is 0.0625.

SOLUTION

Probability that all four tosses are tails: $\left(\frac{1}{2}\right)^4$

Use the power of a quotient property to evaluate.

$$\left(\frac{1}{2}\right)^4 = \frac{1}{2^4} = \frac{1}{16} = 0.0625.$$

The probability of getting four tails is 0.0625.

Exercise for Example 3

7. You toss a fair coin six times. Show that the probability of getting six heads is about 0.0156.

Algebra 1
Practice Workbook with Examples

NAME _____ DATE _____

Practice with Examples

For use with pages 470–475

GOAL Use scientific notation to represent numbers and to describe real-life situations

---

VOCABULARY

A number is written in **scientific notation** if it is of the form $c \times 10^n$, where $1 \leq c < 10$ and n is an integer.

EXAMPLE 1 *Rewriting in Decimal Form*

Rewrite each number in decimal form.

a. 2.23×10^4 **b.** 8.5×10^{-3}

SOLUTION

a. $2.23 \times 10^4 = 22{,}300$ Move decimal point right 4 places.

b. $8.5 \times 10^{-3} = 0.0085$ Move decimal point left 3 places.

Exercises for Example 1

Rewrite each number in decimal form.

1. 9.332×10^6

2. 2.78×10^{-1}

3. 4.5×10^5

Practice with Examples

For use with pages 470–475

EXAMPLE 2 *Rewriting in Scientific Notation*

Rewrite each number in scientific notation.

a. 0.0729   **b.** 26,645

SOLUTION

a. $0.0729 = 7.29 \times 10^{-2}$ Move decimal point right 2 places.

b. $26,645 = 2.6645 \times 10^{4}$ Move decimal point left 4 places.

Exercises for Example 2

Rewrite each number in scientific notation.

4. 75.2   **5.** 135,667   **6.** 0.00088

EXAMPLE 3 *Computing with Scientific Notation*

Evaluate the expression and write the result in scientific notation.

$(7.0 \times 10^{4})^{2}$

SOLUTION

To multiply, divide, or find powers of numbers in scientific notation, use the properties of exponents.

$$(7.0 \times 10^{4})^{2} = 7.0^{2} \times (10^{4})^{2}$$ Power of a product

$$= 49 \times 10^{8}$$ Power of a power

$$= 4.9 \times 10^{9}$$ Write in scientific notation.

Exercises for Example 3

Evaluate the expression and write the result in scientific notation.

7. $(2.3 \times 10^{-1})(5.5 \times 10^{3})$ **8.** $(2.0 \times 10^{-1})^{3}$

NAME _____ DATE _____

Practice with Examples

For use with pages 470–475

EXAMPLE 4 ### Dividing with Scientific Notation

The mass of the sun is approximately 1.99×10^{30} kilograms. The mass of the moon is approximately 7.36×10^{22} kilograms. The mass of the sun is approximately how many times that of the moon?

SOLUTION

Find the ratio of the mass of the sun to the mass of the moon.

$$\frac{1.99 \times 10^{30}}{7.36 \times 10^{22}} \approx 0.27 \times 10^{8}$$

$$= 2.7 \times 10^{7}$$

The mass of the sun is about 27,000,000 times that of the moon.

Exercise for Example 4

9. The Pacific Ocean covers about 1.66241×10^{8} square kilometers. The Baltic Sea covers about 4.144×10^{5} square kilometers. The Pacific Ocean is approximately how many times as large as the Baltic Sea?

Algebra 1
Practice Workbook with Examples

165

Chapter 8

Practice with Examples

For use with pages 477–482

 GOAL Write and use models for exponential growth and graph models for exponential growth

---

VOCABULARY

Exponential growth occurs when a quantity increases by the same percent r in each time period t.

C is the initial amount. ⟶   ⟵ t is the time period.

$$y = C(1 + r)^t$$

The percent of increase is $100r$.   ⟶ $(1 + r)$ is the growth factor, r is the growth rate.

EXAMPLE 1 *Finding the Balance in an Account*

A principal of $600 is deposited in an account that pays 3.5% interest compounded yearly. Find the account balance after 4 years.

SOLUTION

Use the exponential growth model to find the account balance A. The growth rate is 0.035. The initial value is 600.

$A = P(1 + r)^t$	Exponential growth model
$\quad = 600(1 + 0.035)^4$	Substitute 600 for P, 0.035 for r, and 4 for t.
$\quad = 600(1.035)^4$	Simplify.
$\quad \approx 688.514$	Evaluate.

The balance after 4 years will be about $688.51.

Exercises for Example 1

Use the exponential growth model to find the account balance.

1. A principal of $450 is deposited in an account that pays 2.5% interest compounded yearly. Find the account balance after 2 years.

2. A principal of $800 is deposited in an account that pays 3% interest compounded yearly. Find the account balance after 5 years.

Chapter 8

NAME _____ DATE _____

Practice with Examples

For use with pages 477–482

EXAMPLE 2 *Writing an Exponential Growth Model*

A population of 40 pheasants is released in a wildlife preserve.
The population doubles each year for 3 years. What is the population
after 4 years?

SOLUTION

Because the population doubles each year, the growth factor is 2.
Then $1 + r = 2$, and the growth rate $r = 1$.

$$P = C(1 + r)^t \qquad \text{Exponential growth model}$$
$$= 40(1 + 1)^4 \qquad \text{Substitute for } C, r, \text{ and } t.$$
$$= 40 \cdot 2^4 \qquad \text{Simplify.}$$
$$= 640 \qquad \text{Evaluate.}$$

After 4 years, the population will be about 640 pheasants.

Exercise for Example 2

3. A population of 50 pheasants is released in a wildlife preserve.
The population triples each year for 3 years. What is the population
after 3 years?

Chapter 8

NAME _____ DATE _____

Practice with Examples

For use with pages 477–482

EXAMPLE 3 *Graphing an Exponential Growth Model*

Graph the exponential growth model in Example 2.

SOLUTION

Make a table of values, plot the points in a coordinate plane, and draw a smooth curve through the points.

t	0	1	2	3	4	5
P	40	80	160	320	640	1280

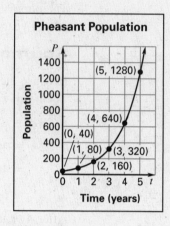

Pheasant Population

Exercise for Example 3

4. Graph the exponential growth model in Exercise 3.

Algebra 1
Practice Workbook with Examples

Chapter 8

Practice with Examples

For use with pages 484–491

GOAL Write and use models for exponential decay and graph models for exponential decay

---

VOCABULARY

Exponential decay occurs when a quantity decreases by the same percent r in each time period t.

C is the initial amount. ⎯⎯⎯   ⎯ t is the time period.

$$y = C(1 - r)^t$$

The percent of decrease is $100r$. $(1 - r)$ is the decay factor, r is the decay rate.

EXAMPLE 1 ## Writing an Exponential Decay Model

You bought a used truck for $15,000. The value of the truck will decrease each year because of depreciation. The truck depreciates at the rate of 8% per year. Write an exponential decay model to represent the real-life problem.

SOLUTION

The initial value C is $15,000. The decay rate r is 0.08. Let y be the value and let t be the number of years you have owned the truck.

$y = C(1 - r)^t$ Exponential decay model

$= 15,000(1 - 0.08)^t$ Substitute 15,000 for C and 0.08 for r.

$= 15,000(0.92)^t$ Simplify.

The exponential decay model is $y = 15,000(0.92)^t$.

Exercises for Example 1

1. Use the exponential decay model in Example 1 to estimate the value of your truck in 5 years.

2. Use the exponential decay model in Example 1 to estimate the value of your truck in 7 years.

3. Rework Example 1 if the truck depreciates at the rate of 10% per year.

Chapter 8

NAME _____ DATE _____

Practice with Examples

For use with pages 484–491

EXAMPLE 2 *Graphing an Exponential Decay Model*

    a. Graph the exponential decay model in Example 1.

    b. Use the graph to estimate the value of your truck in 6 years.

SOLUTION

    a. Make a table of values to verify the model in Example 1. Find
    the value of the truck for each year by multiplying the value in
    the previous year by the decay factor $1 - 0.08 = 0.92$.

Year	Value
0	15,000
1	$0.92(15,000) = 13,800$
2	$0.92(13,800) = 12,696$
3	$0.92(12,696) \approx 11,680$
4	$0.92(11,680) \approx 10,746$
5	$0.92(10,746) \approx 9886$

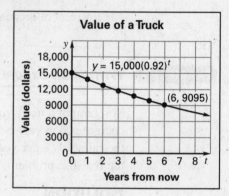

Use the table of values to write ordered pairs:
(0, 15,000), (1, 13,800), (2, 12,696), (3, 11,680),
(4, 10,746), (5, 9886). Plot the points
in a coordinate plane, and draw a smooth curve
through the points.

    b. From the graph, the value of your truck in 6 years is about $9095.

NAME _____ DATE _____

Practice with Examples

For use with pages 484–491

Exercises for Example 2

4. Use the graph in Example 2 to estimate the value of your truck in 8 years.

5. Graph the exponential decay model in Exercise 3.

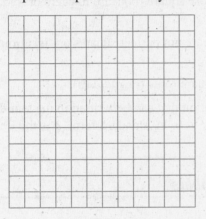

Algebra 1
Practice Workbook with Examples

171

Chapter 8

NAME _____ DATE _____

Practice with Examples

For use with pages 503–510

GOAL Evaluate and approximate square roots and solve a quadratic equation by finding square roots

---

VOCABULARY

If $b^2 = a$, then b is a **square root** of a.

A square root b can be a **positive square root** (or a principal square root) or a **negative square root**.

A **radicand** is the number or expression inside a radical symbol $\sqrt{}$.

Perfect squares are numbers whose square roots are integers or quotients of integers.

The square roots of numbers that are not perfect squares are **irrational numbers**.

A **radical expression** involves square roots (or *radicals*).

A **quadratic equation** is an equation that can be written in the **standard form** $ax^2 + bx + c = 0$, where $a \neq 0$. In standard form, a is the **leading coefficient**.

EXAMPLE 1 *Finding Square Roots of Numbers*

Evaluate the expression.

a. $\sqrt{81}$ **b.** $-\sqrt{49}$ **c.** $\pm\sqrt{0.16}$ **d.** $\sqrt{-1}$

SOLUTION

a. $\sqrt{81} = 9$ Positive square root

b. $-\sqrt{49} = -7$ Negative square root

c. $\pm\sqrt{0.16} = \pm 0.4$ Two square roots

d. $\sqrt{-1}$ (undefined)   No real square root

Exercises for Example 1

Evaluate the expression.

1. $\sqrt{0.09}$

2. $\sqrt{36}$

3. $-\sqrt{25}$

4. $\pm\sqrt{100}$

Algebra 1
Practice Workbook with Examples

NAME _____ DATE _____

Practice with Examples

For use with pages 503–510

EXAMPLE 2 *Evaluating a Radical Expression*

Evaluate $\sqrt{b^2 - 4ac}$ when $a = -2$, $b = -5$, and $c = 2$.

SOLUTION

$$\sqrt{b^2 - 4ac} = \sqrt{(-5)^2 - 4(-2)(2)} \quad \text{Substitute values.}$$
$$= \sqrt{25 + 16} \quad \text{Simplify.}$$
$$= \sqrt{41} \quad \text{Simplify.}$$
$$\approx 6.40 \quad \text{Round to the nearest hundredth.}$$

Exercises for Example 2

Evaluate $\sqrt{b^2 - 4ac}$ **for the given values.**

5. $a = -3, b = 6, c = -3$

6. $a = 1, b = 5, c = 4$

NAME _____ DATE _____

Practice with Examples

For use with pages 503–510

EXAMPLE 3 *Rewriting Before Finding Square Roots*

Solve $4x^2 - 100 = 0$.

SOLUTION

$4x^2 - 100 = 0$	Write original equation.
$4x^2 = 100$	Add 100 to each side.
$x^2 = 25$	Divide each side by 4.
$x = \pm\sqrt{25}$	Find square roots.
$x = \pm 5$	25 is a perfect square.

Exercises for Example 3

Solve the equation or write *no solution*. Write the solutions as integers if possible. Otherwise write them as radical expressions.

7. $6x^2 - 54 = 0$

8. $5x^2 - 15 = 0$

9. $2x^2 - 98 = 0$

Practice with Examples

For use with pages 511–516

GOAL Use properties of radicals to simplify radicals and use quadratic equations to model real-life problems

---

VOCABULARY

Product Property The square root of a product equals the product of the square roots of the factors.

$$\sqrt{ab} = \sqrt{a} \cdot \sqrt{b} \text{ when } a \text{ and } b \text{ are positive numbers}$$

Quotient Property The square root of a quotient equals the quotient of the square roots of the numerator and denominator.

$$\sqrt{\frac{a}{b}} = \frac{\sqrt{a}}{\sqrt{b}} \text{ when } a \text{ and } b \text{ are positive numbers}$$

An expression with radicals is in **simplest form** if the following are true:

• No perfect square factors other than 1 are in the radicand.

• No fractions are in the radicand.

• No radicals appear in the denominator of a fraction.

EXAMPLE 1 *Simplifying with the Product Property*

Simplify the expression $\sqrt{147}$.

SOLUTION

You can use the product property to simplify a radical by removing perfect square factors from the radicand.

$$\sqrt{147} = \sqrt{49 \cdot 3} \qquad \text{Factor using perfect square factor.}$$
$$= \sqrt{49} \cdot \sqrt{3} \qquad \text{Use product property.}$$
$$= 7\sqrt{3} \qquad \text{Simplify.}$$

Exercises for Example 1

Simplify the expression.

1. $\sqrt{98}$

2. $\sqrt{52}$

3. $\sqrt{300}$

4. $\sqrt{99}$

Chapter 9

NAME _____ DATE _____

Practice with Examples

For use with pages 511–516

EXAMPLE 2 *Simplifying with the Quotient Property*

Simplify the expression $\dfrac{\sqrt{63}}{6}$.

SOLUTION

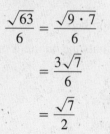

$\dfrac{\sqrt{63}}{6} = \dfrac{\sqrt{9 \cdot 7}}{6}$ Factor using perfect square factor.

$= \dfrac{3\sqrt{7}}{6}$ Remove perfect square factor.

$= \dfrac{\sqrt{7}}{2}$ Divide out common factors.

Exercises for Example 2

Simplify the expression.

5. $\sqrt{\dfrac{11}{4}}$ **6.** $\dfrac{\sqrt{200}}{60}$

7. $\sqrt{\dfrac{5}{9}}$ **8.** $\dfrac{\sqrt{75}}{20}$

Chapter 9

NAME _____ DATE _____

Practice with Examples
For use with pages 511–516

EXAMPLE 3 *Simplifying Radical Expressions*

The speed s (in meters per second) at which a tsunami moves is
determined by the depth d (in meters) of the ocean: $s = \sqrt{gd}$, where g is
9.8 $m/\sec^2$. Find the speed of a tsunami in a region of the ocean that is
2000 meters deep. Write the result in simplified form.

SOLUTION

Write the model for speed of the tsunami and let $d = 2000$ meters.

$$s = \sqrt{gd} \qquad\qquad \text{Write model.}$$
$$= \sqrt{(9.8)(2000)} \qquad \text{Substitute 9.8 for } g \text{ and 2000 for } d.$$
$$= \sqrt{19{,}600} \qquad\qquad \text{Simplify.}$$
$$= \sqrt{196 \cdot 100} \qquad \text{Factor using perfect square factors.}$$
$$= 14 \cdot 10 \qquad\qquad \text{Find square roots.}$$
$$= 140 \qquad\qquad \text{Simplify.}$$

The speed of the tsunami is 140 meters per second.

Exercise for Example 3

9. Rework Example 3 to find the speed of a tsunami in a region of the
   ocean that is 500 meters deep. Write the result in simplified form.

Chapter 9

NAME _____ DATE _____

Practice with Examples

For use with pages 518–524

GOAL Sketch the graph of a quadratic function and use quadratic models in real-life settings

---

VOCABULARY

A **quadratic function** is a function that can be written in the **standard form** $y = ax^2 + bx + c$, where $a \neq 0$.

Every quadratic function has a U-shaped graph called a **parabola.**

The **vertex** of a parabola is the lowest point of a parabola that opens up and the highest point of a parabola that opens down.

The **axis of symmetry** of a parabola is the vertical line passing through the vertex.

EXAMPLE 1 *Sketching a Quadratic Function with a Positive a-value*

Sketch the graph of $y = x^2 - 2x + 1$.

SOLUTION

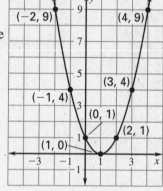

The vertex has an x-coordinate of $-\dfrac{b}{2a}$. Find the x-coordinate when $a = 1$ and $b = -2$.

$$-\frac{b}{2a} = -\frac{-2}{2(1)} = 1$$

Make a table of values, using x-values to the left and right of $x = 1$.

x	-2	-1	0	1	2	3	4
y	9	4	1	0	1	4	9

Plot the points. The vertex is $(1, 0)$ and the axis of symmetry is $x = 1$. Connect the points to form a parabola that opens up because a is positive.

Exercises for Example 1

Sketch the graph of the function. Label the vertex.

1. $y = 2x^2$ **2.** $y = x^2 + 3x$ **3.** $y = x^2 + 2x + 1$

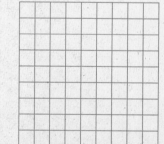

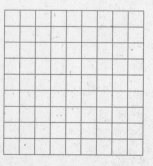

Algebra 1
Practice Workbook with Examples

Practice with Examples

For use with pages 518–524

EXAMPLE 2 *Sketching a Quadratic Function with a Negative a-value*

Sketch the graph of $y = -x^2 + 2x - 3$.

SOLUTION

The vertex has an x-coordinate of $-\dfrac{b}{2a}$. Find the x-coordinate when $a = -1$ and $b = 2$.

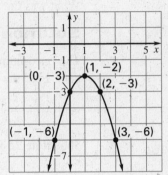

$$-\frac{b}{2a} = -\frac{2}{2(-1)} = 1$$

Make a table of values, using x-values to the left and right of $x = 1$.

x	-1	0	1	2	3
y	-6	-3	-2	-3	-6

Plot the points. The vertex is $(1, -2)$ and the axis of symmetry is $x = 1$. Connect the points to form a parabola that opens down because a is negative.

Exercises for Example 2

Sketch the graph of the function. Label the vertex.

4. $y = -4x^2$

5. $y = -x^2 + x$

6. $y = -x^2 - 2x + 3$

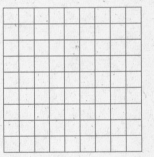

Algebra 1 **179**
Practice Workbook with Examples

Chapter 9

NAME _____ DATE _____

Practice with Examples

For use with pages 518–524

EXAMPLE 3 *Using a Quadratic Model*

A ball was thrown and followed a path described by $y = -0.02x^2 + x$.
What was the maximum height (in feet) of the thrown ball?

SOLUTION

The maximum height of the ball occurred at the vertex of the parabolic
path. Find the x-coordinate of the vertex. Use $a = -0.02$ and $b = 1$.

$$-\frac{b}{2a} = -\frac{1}{2(-0.02)} = \frac{1}{0.04} = 25$$

Substitute 25 for x in the model to find the maximum height.

$$y = -0.02(25)^2 + 25 = 12.5$$

The maximum height of the thrown ball was 12.5 feet.

Exercise for Example 3

7. Rework Example 3 if the path is described by $y = -0.01x^2 + x$.

Chapter 9

NAME _____ DATE _____

Practice with Examples

For use with pages 526–531

GOAL Solve a quadratic equation graphically and use quadratic models in real-life settings

---

VOCABULARY

The solution of a quadratic equation in one variable x can be solved or checked graphically with the following steps.

Step 1: Write the equation in the form $ax^2 + bx + c = 0$.

Step 2: Write the related function $y = ax^2 + bx + c$.

Step 3: Sketch the graph of the function $y = ax^2 + bx + c$. The solutions, or **roots**, of $ax^2 + bx + c = 0$ are the x-intercepts.

EXAMPLE 1 **Checking a Solution Using a Graph**

a. Solve $3x^2 = 75$ algebraically.   **b.** Check your solution graphically.

SOLUTION

a. $3x^2 = 75$ Write original equation.

$x^2 = 25$ Divide each side by 3.

$x = \pm 5$ Find the square root of each side.

b. Write the equation in the form $ax^2 + bx + c = 0$.

$3x^2 = 75$ Write original equation.

$3x^2 - 75 = 0$ Subtract 75 from each side.

Write the related function $y = ax^2 + bx + c$.

$y = 3x^2 - 75$

Sketch the graph of $y = 3x^2 - 75$. The x-intercepts are ± 5, which agrees with the algebraic solution.

Exercises for Example 1

Solve the equation algebraically. Check the solutions graphically.

1. $\frac{1}{3}x^2 = 12$ **2.** $3x^2 + 2 = 50$ **3.** $x^2 - 7 = 2$

NAME _____ DATE _____

Practice with Examples

EXAMPLE 2 **Solving an Equation Graphically**

a. Solve $x^2 - 3x = 4$ graphically.

b. Check your solution algebraically.

SOLUTION

a. Write the equation in the form $ax^2 + bx + c = 0$.

$$x^2 - 3x = 4 \quad \text{Write original equation.}$$

$$x^2 - 3x - 4 = 0 \quad \text{Subtract 4 from each side.}$$

Write the related function $y = ax^2 + bx + c$.

$$y = x^2 - 3x - 4$$

Sketch the graph of the function $y = x^2 - 3x - 4$.

From the graph, the x-intercepts appear to be $x = -1$ and $x = 4$.

b. You can check your solution algebraically by substitution.

Check $x = -1$:   Check $x = 4$:

$$x^2 - 3x = 4 \qquad\qquad x^2 - 3x = 4$$

$$(-1)^2 - 3(-1) \overset{?}{=} 4 \qquad 4^2 - 3(4) \overset{?}{=} 4$$

$$1 + 3 = 4 \qquad\qquad 16 - 12 = 4$$

Exercises for Example 2

Solve the equation graphically. Check the solutions algebraically.

4. $x^2 + x = 12$

5. $x^2 - 5x = -6$

6. $x^2 - 5x = 6$

NAME _____ DATE _____

Practice with Examples

EXAMPLE 3 *Using Quadratic Equations in Real Life*

The average cost of a license and registration for an automobile in the United States from 1991 through 1997 can be modeled by

$$y = -0.63x^2 + 15.08x + 151.57$$

where y represents the average cost of a license and registration. Let x be the number of years since 1990. Use the graph of the model to estimate the average cost of a license and registration in 1995.

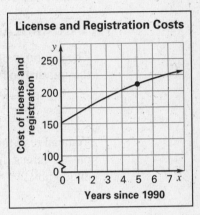

License and Registration Costs

Cost of license and registration

Years since 1990

SOLUTION

The year 1995 corresponds to $x = 5$. From the graph of the quadratic equation, the average cost of a license and registration appears to be about 210 dollars.

Exercise for Example 3

7. Algebraically check the solution in Example 3.

Practice with Examples

For use with pages 533–538

GOAL **Use the quadratic formula to solve a quadratic equation and use quadratic models for real-life situations**

VOCABULARY

The solutions of the quadratic equation $ax^2 + bx + c = 0$ are given by the **quadratic formula**

$$x = \frac{-b \pm \sqrt{b^2 - 4ac}}{2a} \text{ when } a \neq 0 \text{ and } b^2 - 4ac \geq 0.$$

You can read this formula as "x equals the opposite of b, plus or minus the square root of b squared minus $4ac$, all divided by $2a$."

EXAMPLE 1 *Using the Quadratic Formula*

Solve $x^2 + 3x = 4$.

SOLUTION

You must rewrite the equation in standard form $ax^2 + bx + c = 0$ before using the quadratic formula.

$$x^2 + 3x = 4 \qquad \text{Write original equation.}$$

$$x^2 + 3x - 4 = 0 \qquad \text{Rewrite equation in standard form.}$$

$$1x^2 + 3x + (-4) = 0 \qquad \text{Identify } a = 1, b = 3, \text{ and } c = -4.$$

$$x = \frac{-3 \pm \sqrt{3^2 - 4(1)(-4)}}{2(1)} \qquad \begin{array}{l}\text{Substitute values into the quadratic} \\ \text{formula: } a = 1, b = 3, \text{ and } c = -4.\end{array}$$

$$x = \frac{-3 \pm \sqrt{9 + 16}}{2} \qquad \text{Simplify.}$$

$$x = \frac{-3 \pm \sqrt{25}}{2} \qquad \text{Simplify.}$$

$$x = \frac{-3 \pm 5}{2} \qquad \text{Solutions.}$$

The equation has two solutions:

$$x = \frac{-3 + 5}{2} = 1 \text{ and } x = \frac{-3 - 5}{2} = -4$$

Algebra 1
Practice Workbook with Examples

NAME _____ DATE _____

Practice with Examples

For use with pages 533–538

Exercises for Example 1

Use the quadratic formula to solve the equation.

1. $x^2 - 4x + 3 = 0$ **2.** $x^2 + 9x + 20 = 0$ **3.** $x^2 + x = 6$

EXAMPLE 2   *Modeling Vertical Motion*

You retrieve a football from a tree 25 feet above ground. You throw it downward with an initial speed of 20 feet per second. Use a vertical motion model to find how long it will take for the football to reach the ground.

SOLUTION

Because the football is thrown down, the initial velocity is $v = -20$ feet per second. The initial height is $s = 25$ feet. The football will reach the ground when the height is 0.

$h = -16t^2 + vt + s$	Choose the vertical motion model for a thrown object.
$h = -16t^2 + (-20)t + 25$	Substitute values for v and s into the vertical motion model.
$0 = -16t^2 - 20t + 25$	Substitute 0 for h.
$t = \dfrac{-(-20) \pm \sqrt{(-20)^2 - 4(-16)(25)}}{2(-16)}$	Substitute values into the quadratic formula: $a = -16$, $b = -20$, and $c = 25$.
$t = \dfrac{20 \pm \sqrt{2000}}{-32}$	Simplify.
$t \approx 0.773$ or -2.023	Solutions

The football will reach the ground about 0.773 seconds after it was thrown. As a solution, -2.023 doesn't make sense in the problem.

NAME _____ DATE _____

Practice with Examples

For use with pages 533–538

Exercises for Example 2

4. Rework Example 3 if the football is dropped from the tree with an initial speed of 0 feet per second.

NAME _____ DATE _____

Practice with Examples

For use with pages 541–547

GOAL **Use the discriminant to find the number of solutions of a quadratic equation and apply the discriminant to solve real-life problems**

VOCABULARY

The **discriminant** is the expression inside the radical in the quadratic formula, $b^2 - 4ac$.

Consider the quadratic equation $ax^2 + bx + c = 0$.

- If $b^2 - 4ac$ is positive, then the equation has two solutions.
- If $b^2 - 4ac$ is zero, then the equation has one solution.
- If $b^2 - 4ac$ is negative, then the equation has no real solution.

EXAMPLE 1 *Finding the Number of Solutions*

Find the value of the discriminant and use the value to tell if the equation has *two solutions*, *one solution*, or *no solution*.

  a. $3x^2 - 2x - 1 = 0$ **b.** $x^2 - 8x + 16 = 0$ **c.** $x^2 - 4x + 5 = 0$

SOLUTION

  a. $b^2 - 4ac = (-2)^2 - 4(3)(-1)$ Substitute 3 for a, -2 for b, -1 for c.

               $= 4 + 12$ Simplify.

               $= 16$ Discriminant is positive.

    The discriminant is positive, so the equation has two solutions.

  b. $b^2 - 4ac = (-8)^2 - 4(1)(16)$ Substitute 1 for a, -8 for b, 16 for c.

               $= 64 - 64$ Simplify

               $= 0$ Discriminant is zero.

    The discriminant is zero, so the equation has one solution.

  c. $b^2 - 4ac = (-4)^2 - 4(1)(5)$ Substitute 1 for a, -4 for b, 5 for c.

               $= 16 - 20$ Simplify.

               $= -4$ Discriminant is negative.

    The discriminant is negative, so the equation has no solution.

Chapter 9

NAME _____ DATE _____

Practice with Examples

For use with pages 541–547

Exercises for Example 1

Tell if the equation has two solutions, one solution, or no solution.

1. $x^2 - 10x + 25 = 0$ **2.** $2x^2 - x - 1 = 0$ **3.** $x^2 + 2x + 4 = 0$

4. $-x^2 + 6x - 9 = 0$ **5.** $-2x^2 - 5x - 4 = 0$ **6.** $3x^2 + 2x - 16 = 0$

EXAMPLE 2 *Using the Discriminant in a Real-Life Problem*

You work as an accountant for a sporting goods company. You have been asked to project the revenue of the company. The revenue of the company from 1990 to 1995 can be modeled by

$$R = 1.23t^2 - 2.22t + 8.5$$

where R is the revenue in millions of dollars and t is the number of years since 1990. Use the model to predict whether the revenue will reach 90 million dollars.

SOLUTION

Set the revenue model equal to 90 and use the discriminant to determine the number of solutions of the quadratic revenue model.

$R = 1.23t^2 - 2.22t + 8.5$	Write revenue model.
$90 = 1.23t^2 - 2.22t + 8.5$	Substitute 90 for R.
$0 = 1.23t^2 - 2.22t - 81.5$	Rewrite equation in standard form.
$0 = 1.23t^2 + (-2.22)t + (-81.5)$	Identify $a = 1.23$, $b = -2.22$, and $c = -81.5$.
$b^2 - 4ac = (-2.22)^2 - 4(1.23)(-81.5)$	Substitute 1.23 for a, -2.22 for b, -81.5 for c.
$= 4.9284 + 400.98$	Simplify.
$= 405.9084$	Discriminant is positive.

The discriminant is positive, so the equation has two solutions. You predict that the company's revenue will reach 90 million dollars.

Algebra 1
Practice Workbook with Examples

Chapter 9

NAME _____ DATE _____

Practice with Examples

For use with pages 541–547

Exercises for Example 2

7. Use the discriminant to show that the revenue for the company will reach $150 million.

8. Use a graphing calculator to find how many years it will take for the revenue to reach $90 million.

Chapter 9

LESSON 9.7

Practice with Examples

For use with pages 548–553

GOAL **Sketch the graph of a quadratic inequality**

> ### VOCABULARY
>
> The following are types of **quadratic inequalities.**
>
> $y < ax^2 + bx + c$ $y \leq ax^2 + bx + c$
>
> $y > ax^2 + bx + c$ $y \geq ax^2 + bx + c$
>
> The **graph** of a quadratic inequality consists of the graph of all ordered pairs (x, y) that are solutions of the inequality.

EXAMPLE 1 **Checking Solutions**

Decide whether the ordered pairs $(-4, -5)$ and $(0, 2)$ are solutions of the inequality $y < x^2 + 5x$.

SOLUTION

$y < x^2 + 5x$ Write original inequality.

$-5 \overset{?}{<} (-4)^2 + 5(-4)$ Substitute -4 for x and -5 for y.

$-5 < -4$ True.

Because $-5 < -4$, the ordered pair $(-4, -5)$ is a solution of the inequality.

$y < x^2 + 5x$ Write original inequality.

$2 \overset{?}{<} (0)^2 + 5(0)$ Substitute 0 for x and 2 for y.

$2 \not< 0$ False.

Because $2 \not< 0$, the ordered pair $(0, 2)$ is not a solution of the inequality.

Exercises for Example 1

Decide whether the ordered pair is a solution of the inequality.

1. $y \geq x^2 - 2x, (2, 0)$

2. $y < 2x^2 + x, (1, -1)$

3. $y > x^2 - 3x, (2, -3)$

Chapter 9

NAME _____ DATE _____

Practice with Examples

For use with pages 548–553

EXAMPLE 2 *Graphing a Quadratic Inequality*

Sketch the graph of $y \geq 2x^2 + 6x$.

SOLUTION

Sketch the parabola $y = 2x^2 + 6x$ using a solid line because the inequality is $\geq$. The parabola opens up. Test the point $(2, 0)$ which is not on the parabola.

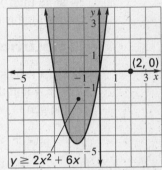

$$y \geq 2x^2 + 6x \qquad \text{Write original inequality.}$$

$$0 \overset{?}{\geq} 2(2)^2 + 6(2) \qquad \text{Substitute 2 for } x \text{ and 0 for } y.$$

$$0 \not\geq 20 \qquad \text{False.}$$

Because 0 is not greater than or equal to 20, the ordered pair $(2, 0)$ is not a solution.

The point $(2, 0)$ is not a solution and it is outside the parabola, so the graph of $y \geq 2x^2 + 6x$ is all the points inside or on the parabola.

Exercises for Example 2

Sketch the graph of the inequality.

4. $y \leq x^2 + 4x + 4$ **5.** $y \geq 3x^2 - 12$ **6.** $y \leq x^2 - 10x + 9$

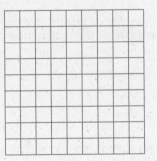

NAME _____ DATE _____

Practice with Examples

For use with pages 548–553

EXAMPLE 3 *Using a Quadratic Inequality Model*

A rectangular pen is 4 feet longer than it is wide. The area of the pen is more than 32 square feet. Sketch the inequality that describes the possible dimensions of the pen.

SOLUTION

Let x represent the width of the pen. So, the pen's length is $x + 4$ and the area of the pen is $x(x + 4)$. Since the area of the pen is greater than 32 square feet, you have

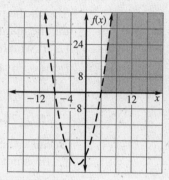

$$x(x + 4) > 32$$

$$x^2 + 4x > 32$$

$$x^2 + 4x - 32 > 0.$$

Sketch the parabola using a dashed line. The parabola opens up. Test the point $(0, 0)$ to determine what portion of the graph to shade. Since the point $(0, 0)$ does not satisfy the inequality, the graph of $x^2 + 4x - 32 > 0$ is all the points outside the parabola. Since the length cannot be negative, only points in the first quadrant are considered. So, the width should be greater than 4 feet and the length greater than 8 feet.

Exercises for Example 3

7. Give two possible scenarios for the dimensions of the rectangular pen in Example 3.

8. Suppose a rectangular pen is 10 feet longer than it is wide and its area is more than 96 square feet. Sketch the inequality that describes the dimensions of the rectangular pen.

Algebra 1
Practice Workbook with Examples

Practice with Examples

For use with pages 554–560

GOAL **Choose a model that best fits a collection of data and use models in real-life settings**

VOCABULARY

Linear Model	Exponential Model	Quadratic Model
$y = mx + b$	$y = C(1 \pm r)^t$	$y = ax^2 + bx + c$

EXAMPLE 1 *Choosing a Model*

Name the type of model that best fits each data collection.

a. $\left(-2, \frac{1}{4}\right), \left(-1, \frac{1}{2}\right), (0, 1), (1, 2), (2, 4)$

b. $(-2, -3), (-1, -1), (0, 1), (1, 3), (2, 5)$

c. $(-2, 5), (-1, 2), (0, 1), (1, 2), (2, 5)$

SOLUTION

Make scatter plots of the data. Then decide whether the points lie on a line, an exponential curve, or a parabola.

a. Exponential Model   **b.** Linear Model   **c.** Quadratic Model

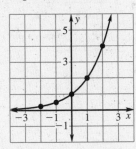   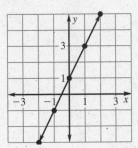   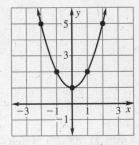

Exercises for Example 1

Make a scatter plot of the data. Then name the type of model that best fits the data.

1. $(-2, 3), (-1, 0), (0, -1), (1, 0), (2, 3)$

NAME _____ DATE _____

Practice with Examples

For use with pages 554–560

2. $(-2, -3), (-1, -2), (0, -1), (1, 0), (2, 1)$

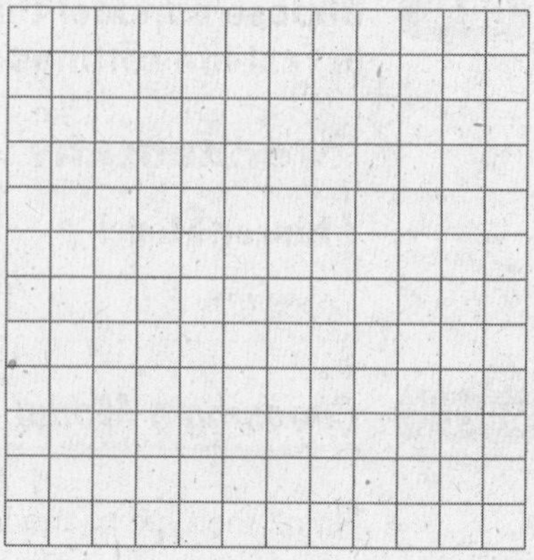

3. $(-2, 4), (-1, 2), (0, 1), \left(1, \frac{1}{2}\right), \left(2, \frac{1}{4}\right)$

EXAMPLE 2 **Writing a Model**

Your biology class is studying the population growth of fruit flies. The table shows the population, P (number of fruit flies) for various times, t (in weeks). Which type of model best fits the data?

t	0	1	2	3	4
P	2	6	18	54	162

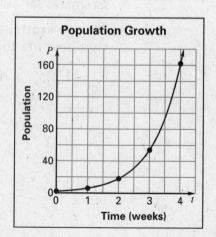

Population Growth

Algebra 1
Practice Workbook with Examples

Chapter 9

Practice with Examples

For use with pages 554–560

SOLUTION

Draw a scatter plot of the data. You can see that the graph is curved, not linear. Test whether a quadratic model fits. Begin by writing the simple quadratic model $P = at^2$. To find a, substitute any known values of P and t.

$P = at^2$	Write quadratic model.
$6 = a \cdot 1^2$	Substitute 6 for P and 1 for t.
$6 = a$	Solve for a.
$P = 6t^2$	Substitute 6 for a in the equation.

Now check several values of t in the quadratic model $P = 6t^2$.

$$P = 6t^2 \qquad\qquad P = 6t^2$$
$$P = 6(2)^2 \qquad\quad P = 6(4)^2$$
$$P = 24 \neq 18 \qquad P = 96 \neq 162$$

The quadratic model does not fit the data. You can test whether an exponential model fits the data by finding the ratios of consecutive populations.

$$\frac{\text{Population Week } 0}{\text{Population Week } 1} = \frac{2}{6} = \frac{1}{3}$$

$$\frac{\text{Population Week } 1}{\text{Population Week } 2} = \frac{6}{18} = \frac{1}{3}$$

Because the populations increase by the same percent, an exponential model fits the data.

Exercise for Example 2

4. Which type of model best fits the data?

t	0	1	2	3	4
P	2	3	6	11	18

Copyright © McDougal Littell Inc.
All rights reserved.

Algebra 1
Practice Workbook with Examples

195

Chapter 9

NAME _____ DATE _____

Practice with Examples

For use with pages 576–582

GOAL Add and subtract polynomials and use polynomials to model real-life situations

---

VOCABULARY

A **polynomial** is an expression whose terms are of the form ax^k where k is a non-negative integer.

A polynomial is written in **standard form** when the terms are placed in descending order, from largest degree to smallest degree.

The **degree** of each term of a polynomial is the exponent of the variable.

The **degree of a polynomial** is the largest degree of its terms.

When a polynomial is written in standard form, the coefficient of the first term is the **leading coefficient.**

A **monomial** is a polynomial with only one term.

A **binomial** is a polynomial with two terms.

A **trinomial** is a polynomial with three terms.

EXAMPLE 1 *Adding Polynomials*

Find the sum and write the answer in standard form.

a. $(6x - x^2 + 3) + (4x^2 - x - 2)$

b. $(x^2 - x - 4) + (2x + 3x^2 + 1)$

SOLUTION

a. Vertical format: Write each expression in standard form. Align like terms.

$$-x^2 + 6x + 3$$
$$\underline{4x^2 - x - 2}$$
$$3x^2 + 5x + 1$$

b. Horizontal format: Add like terms.

$$(x^2 - x - 4) + (2x + 3x^2 + 1) = (x^2 + 3x^2) + (-x + 2x) + (-4 + 1)$$
$$= 4x^2 + x - 3$$

Practice with Examples

For use with pages 576–582

Exercises for Example 1

Find the sum.

1. $(7 + 2x - 4x^2) + (-3x + x^2 - 5)$ **2.** $(8x - 9 + 2x^2) + (1 + x - 6x^2)$

EXAMPLE 2   *Subtracting Polynomials*

Find the difference and write the answer in standard form.

a. $(5x^2 - 4x + 1) - (8 - x^2)$ **b.** $(-x + 2x^2) - (3x^2 + 7x - 2)$

SOLUTION

a. Vertical format: To subtract, you add the opposite.

$$
\begin{array}{lll}
\quad(5x^2 - 4x + 1) & & 5x^2 - 4x + 1 \\
- \qquad (8 - x^2) & \text{Add the opposite.} & \underline{+\ x^2 \qquad\ \ - 8} \\
& & 6x^2 - 4x - 7
\end{array}
$$

b. Horizontal format:

$$
\begin{aligned}
(-x + 2x^2) - (3x^2 + 7x - 2) &= -x + 2x^2 - 3x^2 - 7x + 2 \\
&= (2x^2 - 3x^2) + (-x - 7x) + 2 \\
&= -x^2 - 8x + 2
\end{aligned}
$$

Exercises for Example 2

Find the difference.

3. $(x + 7x^2) - (1 + 3x - x^2)$

4. $(2x + 3 - 5x^2) - (2x^2 - x + 6)$

Practice with Examples

For use with pages 576–582

EXAMPLE 3 *Using Polynomials in Real-Life*

From 1992 to 1996, the annual sales (in millions of dollars) for Company
D and Company S can be modeled by the following equations, where t is
the number of years since 1992.

Company D: $D = 316t^2 - 1138t + 3145$

Company S: $S = 127t^2 - 155t + 3452$

Find a model for the total annual sales A (in millions of dollars) for
Company D and Company S from 1992 to 1996.

SOLUTION

You can find a model for A by adding the models for D and S.

$$316t^2 - 1138t + 3145$$
$$+ \; 127t^2 - \;\; 155t + 3452$$
$$\overline{443t^2 - 1293t + 6597}$$

The model for the sum is $A = 443t^2 - 1293t + 6597$.

Exercise for Example 3

5. Find a model for the difference N (in millions of dollars) of Company
   D sales and Company S sales from 1992 to 1996.

LESSON
10.2

Practice with Examples

For use with pages 584–589

GOAL Multiply two polynomials and use polynomial multiplication in real-life situations.

VOCABULARY

To multiply two binomials, use a pattern called the **FOIL** pattern. Multiply the First, Outer, Inner, and Last terms.

EXAMPLE 1 ## *Multiplying Binomials Using the FOIL Pattern*

Find the product $(4x + 3)(x + 2)$.

SOLUTION

$$\overset{\text{F O I L}}{(4x + 3)(x + 2) = 4x^2 + 8x + 3x + 6} \qquad \text{Mental math}$$
$$= 4x^2 + 11x + 6 \qquad \text{Simplify.}$$

Exercises for Example 1

Use the FOIL pattern to find the product.

1. $(2x + 3)(x + 1)$

2. $(y - 2)(y - 3)$

3. $(3a + 2)(2a - 1)$

NAME _____ DATE _____

Practice with Examples

For use with pages 584–589

EXAMPLE 2 *Multiplying Polynomials Vertically*

Find the product $(x + 3)(4 - 2x^2 + x)$.

SOLUTION

To multiply two polynomials that have three or more terms, you must multiply each term of one polynomial by each term of the other polynomial. Align like terms in columns.

$$
\begin{array}{llll}
-2x^2 + & x + & 4 & \quad \text{Standard form} \\
& x + & 3 & \quad \text{Standard form} \\
\hline
-6x^2 + & 3x + & 12 & \quad 3(-2x^2 + x + 4) \\
-2x^3 + & x^2 + 4x & & \quad x(-2x^2 + x + 4) \\
\hline
-2x^3 - & 5x^2 + 7x + & 12 & \quad \text{Combine like terms.}
\end{array}
$$

Exercises for Example 2

Multiply the polynomials vertically.

4. $(a + 4)(a^2 + 3 - 2a)$

5. $(2y + 1)(y^2 - 5 + y)$

EXAMPLE 3 *Multiplying Polynomials Horizontally*

Find the product $(x + 4)(-2x^2 + 3x - 1)$.

SOLUTION

Multiply $-2x^2 + 3x - 1$ by each term of $x + 4$.

$$
\begin{aligned}
(x + 4)(-2x^2 + 3x - 1) &= x(-2x^2 + 3x - 1) + 4(-2x^2 + 3x - 1) \\
&= -2x^3 + 3x^2 - x - 8x^2 + 12x - 4 \\
&= -2x^3 - 5x^2 + 11x - 4
\end{aligned}
$$

Algebra 1
Practice Workbook with Examples

NAME _____ DATE _____

Practice with Examples

For use with pages 584–589

Exercises for Example 3

Multiply the polynomials horizontally.

6. $(a + 4)(a^2 + 3 - 2a)$ **7.** $(2y + 1)(y^2 - 5 + y)$

EXAMPLE 4   *Multiplying Binomials to Find an Area*

The dimensions of a rectangular garden can be represented by a width of $(x + 6)$ feet and a length of $(2x + 5)$ feet. Write a polynomial expression for the area A of the garden.

SOLUTION

The area model for a rectangle is $A = $ (width)(length).

$$
\begin{aligned}
A &= \text{(width)(length)} && \text{Area model for a rectangle} \\
&= (x + 6)(2x + 5) && \text{Substitute } x + 6 \text{ for width and } 2x + 5 \text{ for length.} \\
&= 2x^2 + 5x + 12x + 30 && \text{FOIL pattern} \\
&= 2x^2 + 17x + 30 && \text{Combine like terms.}
\end{aligned}
$$

The area A of the garden can be represented by $2x^2 + 17x + 30$ square feet.

Exercise for Example 4

8. Rework Example 4 if the width is $(x + 3)$ feet and the length is $(3x + 2)$ feet.

Practice with Examples

For use with pages 590–596

GOAL   Use special product patterns for the product of a sum and a difference and for the square of a binomial and use special products in real-life models

---

VOCABULARY

Some pairs of binomials have **special product** patterns as follows.

Sum and Difference Pattern
$$(a + b)(a - b) = a^2 - b^2$$

Square of a Binomial Pattern
$$(a + b)^2 = a^2 + 2ab + b^2$$
$$(a - b)^2 = a^2 - 2ab + b^2$$

EXAMPLE 1   *Using the Sum and Difference Pattern*

Use the sum and difference pattern to find the product $(4y + 3)(4y - 3)$.

SOLUTION

$(a + b)(a - b) = a^2 - b^2$	Write pattern.
$(4y + 3)(4y - 3) = (4y)^2 - 3^2$	Apply pattern.
$= 16y^2 - 9$	Simplify.

Exercises for Example 1

Use the sum and difference pattern to find the product.

1. $(x + 5)(x - 5)$ **2.** $(3x + 2)(3x - 2)$

3. $(x + 2y)(x - 2y)$

Algebra 1
Practice Workbook with Examples

NAME _____ DATE _____

Practice with Examples

For use with pages 590–596

EXAMPLE 2 *Squaring a Binomial*

Use the square of a binomial pattern to find the product.

a. $(2x + 3)^2$ **b.** $(4x - 1)^2$

SOLUTION

a. $(a + b)^2 = a^2 + 2ab + b^2$ Write pattern.

$(2x + 3)^2 = (2x)^2 + 2(2x)(3) + 3^2$ Apply pattern.

$= 4x^2 + 12x + 9$ Simplify.

b. $(a - b)^2 = a^2 - 2ab + b^2$ Write pattern.

$(4x - 1)^2 = (4x)^2 - 2(4x)(1) + 1^2$ Apply pattern.

$= 16x^2 - 8x + 1$ Simplify.

Exercises for Example 2

Use the square of a binomial pattern to find the product.

4. $(m + n)^2$ **5.** $(3x - 2)^2$

6. $(7y + 2)^2$

NAME _____ DATE _____

Practice with Examples

For use with pages 590–596

EXAMPLE 3 *Applying a Special Product Pattern to Find an Area*
_____

Use a special product pattern to find an expression for the area of the shaded region.

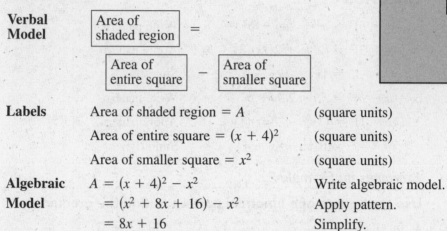

SOLUTION

Verbal Model

Area of shaded region	=

Area of entire square	−	Area of smaller square

Labels

Area of shaded region = A (square units)

Area of entire square = $(x + 4)^2$ (square units)

Area of smaller square = x^2 (square units)

Algebraic Model

$A = (x + 4)^2 - x^2$ Write algebraic model.

$= (x^2 + 8x + 16) - x^2$ Apply pattern.

$= 8x + 16$ Simplify.

The area of the shaded region can be represented by $8x + 16$ square units.

Exercises for Example 3
....

7. Use a special product pattern to find an expression for the area of the shaded region.

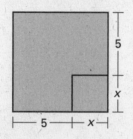

8. Use a special product pattern to find an expression for the area of the shaded region.

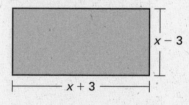

NAME _____ DATE _____

Practice with Examples

For use with pages 597–602

GOAL Solve a polynomial equation in factored form and relate factors and *x*-intercepts

VOCABULARY

A polynomial is in **factored form** if it is written as the product of two or more linear factors. According to the **zero-product property,** if the product of two factors is zero, then at least one of the factors must be zero.

EXAMPLE 1 *Using the Zero-Product Property*

Solve the equation $(x - 1)(x + 7) = 0$.

SOLUTION

Use the zero-product property: either $x - 1 = 0$ or $x + 7 = 0$.

$(x - 1)(x + 7) = 0$	Write original equation.
$x - 1 = 0$	Set first factor equal to 0.
$x = 1$	Solve for x.
$x + 7 = 0$	Set second factor equal to 0.
$x = -7$	Solve for x.

The solutions are 1 and -7.

Exercises for Example 1

Solve the equation.

1. $(z - 6)(z + 6) = 0$

2. $(y - 5)(y - 1) = 0$

3. $(x + 4)(x + 3) = 0$

NAME _____ DATE _____

LESSON 10.4 CONTINUED

Practice with Examples

For use with pages 597–602

EXAMPLE 2 *Using the Zero-Product Property*

Solve the equation $(x - 4)^2 = 0$.

SOLUTION

This equation has a repeated factor. To solve the equation you only need to set $x - 4$ equal to zero.

$$(x - 4)^2 = 0 \qquad \text{Write original equation.}$$
$$x - 4 = 0 \qquad \text{Set repeated factor equal to 0.}$$
$$x = 4 \qquad \text{Solve for } x.$$

The solution is 4.

Exercises for Example 2

Solve the equation.

4. $(t - 5)^2 = 0$

5. $(y + 3)^2 = 0$

6. $(2x + 4)^2 = 0$

Algebra 1
Practice Workbook with Examples

NAME _____ DATE _____

Practice with Examples

For use with pages 597–602

EXAMPLE 3 *Relating x-Intercepts and Factors*

Name the *x*-intercepts and the vertex of the graph
of the function $y = (x + 4)(x - 2)$. Then sketch
the graph of the function.

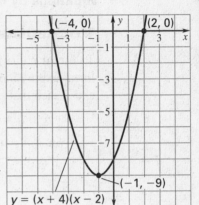

SOLUTION

First solve $(x + 4)(x - 2) = 0$ to find the
x-intercepts: -4 and 2.

Then find the coordinates of the vertex.

- The *x*-coordinate of the vertex is the average
  of the *x*-intercepts.

$$x = \frac{-4 + 2}{2} = -1$$

- Substitute to find the *y*-coordinate.

$$y = (-1 + 4)(-1 - 2) = -9$$

- The coordinates of the vertex are $(-1, -9)$.

Exercises for Example 3

**Name the *x*-intercepts and the vertex of the graph of the
function.**

7. $y = (x + 3)(x + 1)$

8. $y = (x - 2)(x - 4)$

9. $y = (x - 1)(x + 5)$

NAME _____ DATE _____

Practice with Examples

For use with pages 604–609

GOAL Factor a quadratic expression of the form $x^2 + bx + c$ and solve quadratic equations by factoring

> ### VOCABULARY
>
> To **factor** a quadratic expression means to write it as the product of two linear expressions. To factor $x^2 + bx + c$, you need to find numbers p and q such that
>
> $$p + q = b \quad \text{and} \quad pq = c.$$
>
> $x^2 + bx + c = (x + p)(x + q)$ when $p + q = b$ and $pq = c$

EXAMPLE 1 *Factoring when b and c are Positive*

Factor $x^2 + 6x + 8$.

SOLUTION

For this trinomial, $b = 6$ and $c = 8$. You need to find two numbers whose sum is 6 and whose product is 8.

$$x^2 + 6x + 8 = (x + p)(x + q) \quad \text{Find } p \text{ and } q \text{ when } p + q = 6 \text{ and } pq = 8.$$
$$= (x + 4)(x + 2) \quad p = 4 \text{ and } q = 2$$

Exercises for Example 1

Factor the trinomial.

1. $x^2 + 5x + 6$

2. $x^2 + 6x + 5$

3. $x^2 + 3x + 2$

Algebra 1
Practice Workbook with Examples

NAME _____ DATE _____

Practice with Examples

For use with pages 604–609

EXAMPLE 2 *Factoring when b is Negative and c is Positive*

Factor $x^2 - 5x + 4$.

SOLUTION

Because b is negative and c is positive, both p and q must be negative numbers. Find two numbers whose sum is -5 and whose product is 4.

$$x^2 - 5x + 4 = (x + p)(x + q) \qquad \text{Find } p \text{ and } q \text{ when } p + q = -5 \text{ and } pq = 4.$$
$$= (x - 4)(x - 1) \qquad p = -4 \text{ and } q = -1$$

Exercises for Example 2

Factor the trinomial.

4. $x^2 - 3x + 2$ **5.** $x^2 - 7x + 12$ **6.** $x^2 - 5x + 6$

EXAMPLE 3 *Factoring when b and c are Negative*

Factor $x^2 - 3x - 10$.

SOLUTION

For this trinomial, $b = -3$ and $c = -10$. Because c is negative, you know that p and q cannot both have negative values.

$$x^2 - 3x - 10 = (x + p)(x + q) \qquad \text{Find } p \text{ and } q \text{ when } p + q = -3 \text{ and } pq = -10.$$
$$= (x + 2)(x - 5) \qquad p = 2 \text{ and } q = -5$$

Exercises for Example 3

Factor the trinomial.

7. $x^2 - x - 2$ **8.** $x^2 - 4x - 12$ **9.** $x^2 - 2x - 8$

Practice with Examples

For use with pages 604–609

EXAMPLE 4 *Solving a Quadratic Equation*

Solve $x^2 + 4x = 12$.

SOLUTION

$x^2 + 4x = 12$	Write equation.
$x^2 + 4x - 12 = 0$	Write in standard form.
$(x + 6)(x - 2) = 0$	Factor left side. Because c is negative, p and q cannot both have negative values: $p = 6$ and $q = -2$
$(x + 6) = 0$ or $(x - 2) = 0$	Use zero-product property.
$x + 6 = 0$	Set first factor equal to 0.
$x = -6$	Solve for x.
$x - 2 = 0$	Set second factor equal to 0.
$x = 2$	Solve for x.

The solutions are -6 and 2.

Exercises for Example 4

Solve the equation.

10. $x^2 + 8x + 15 = 0$

11. $x^2 - 8x + 12 = 0$

12. $x^2 + 3x - 4 = 0$

Algebra 1
Practice Workbook with Examples

Practice with Examples

For use with pages 611–617

GOAL Factor a quadratic expression of the form $ax^2 + bx + c$ and solve quadratic equations by factoring

VOCABULARY

To factor quadratic polynomials whose leading coefficient is not 1, find the factors of a (m and n) and the factors of c (p and q) so that the sum of the outer and inner products (mq and pn) is b.

$$c = pq$$
$$ax^2 + bx + c = (mx + p)(nx + q) \qquad b = mq + pn$$
$$a = mn$$

EXAMPLE 1 *One Pair of Factors for a and c*

Factor $3x^2 + 7x + 2$.

SOLUTION

Test the possible factors of a (1 and 3) and c (1 and 2).

Try $a = 1 \cdot 3$ and $c = 1 \cdot 2$.

$\qquad (1x + 1)(3x + 2) = 3x^2 + 5x + 2 \qquad$ Not correct

Try $a = 1 \cdot 3$ and $c = 2 \cdot 1$.

$\qquad (1x + 2)(3x + 1) = 3x^2 + 7x + 2 \qquad$ Correct

The correct factorization of $3x^2 + 7x + 2$ is $(x + 2)(3x + 1)$.

Exercises for Example 1

Factor the trinomial.

1. $5x^2 + 11x + 2$ **2.** $2x^2 + 5x + 3$ **3.** $3x^2 + 10x + 7$

Practice with Examples

For use with pages 611–617

EXAMPLE 2 *Several Pairs of Factors for a and c*

Factor $4x^2 - 13x + 10$.

SOLUTION

Both factors of c must be negative, because b is negative and c is positive.

Test the possible factors of a and c.

FACTORS OF a and c	PRODUCT	CORRECT?
$a = 1 \cdot 4$ and $c = (-1)(-10)$	$(x - 1)(4x - 10) = 4x^2 - 14x + 10$	No
$a = 1 \cdot 4$ and $c = (-10)(-1)$	$(x - 10)(4x - 1) = 4x^2 - 41x + 10$	No
$a = 1 \cdot 4$ and $c = (-2)(-5)$	$(x - 2)(4x - 5) = 4x^2 - 13x + 10$	Yes
$a = 1 \cdot 4$ and $c = (-5)(-2)$	$(x - 5)(4x - 2) = 4x^2 - 22x + 10$	No
$a = 2 \cdot 2$ and $c = (-1)(-10)$	$(2x - 1)(2x - 10) = 4x^2 - 22x + 10$	No
$a = 2 \cdot 2$ and $c = (-10)(-1)$	$(2x - 10)(2x - 1) = 4x^2 - 22x + 10$	No
$a = 2 \cdot 2$ and $c = (-2)(-5)$	$(2x - 2)(2x - 5) = 4x^2 - 14x + 10$	No
$a = 2 \cdot 2$ and $c = (-5)(-2)$	$(2x - 5)(2x - 2) = 4x^2 - 14x + 10$	No

The correct factorization of $4x^2 - 13x + 10$ is $(x - 2)(4x - 5)$.

Exercises for Example 2

Factor the trinomial.

4. $9x^2 + 65x + 14$

5. $6x^2 - 23x + 15$

6. $8x^2 + 38x + 9$

NAME _____ DATE _____

Practice with Examples

For use with pages 611–617

EXAMPLE 3 *Solving a Quadratic Equation*

Solve the equation $3x^2 - x = 10$ by factoring.

SOLUTION

$3x^2 - x = 10$	Write equation.
$3x^2 - x - 10 = 0$	Write in standard form.
$(3x + 5)(x - 2) = 0$	Factor left side.
$(3x + 5) = 0 \text{ or } (x - 2) = 0$	Use zero-product property.
$3x + 5 = 0$	Set first factor equal to 0.
$x = -\frac{5}{3}$	Solve for x.
$x - 2 = 0$	Set second factor equal to 0.
$x = 2$	Solve for x.

The solutions are $-\frac{5}{3}$ and 2.

Exercises for Example 3

Solve the equation by factoring.

7. $2x^2 + 7x + 3 = 0$

8. $5n^2 - 17n = -6$

9. $6x^2 - x - 2 = 0$

NAME _____ DATE _____

Practice with Examples

For use with pages 619–624

GOAL Use special product patterns to factor quadratic polynomials and solve quadratic equations by factoring

---

VOCABULARY

Factoring Special Products

Difference of Two Squares Pattern   **Example**

$a^2 - b^2 = (a + b)(a - b)$ $9x^2 - 16 = (3x + 4)(3x - 4)$

Perfect Square Trinomial Pattern   **Example**

$a^2 + 2ab + b^2 = (a + b)^2$ $x^2 + 8x + 16 = (x + 4)^2$

$a^2 - 2ab + b^2 = (a - b)^2$ $x^2 - 12x + 36 = (x - 6)^2$

EXAMPLE 1 *Factoring the Difference of Two Squares*

a. $n^2 - 25$ **b.** $4x^2 - y^2$

SOLUTION

a. $n^2 - 25 = n^2 - 5^2$ Write as $a^2 - b^2$.

$= (n + 5)(n - 5)$ Factor using difference of two squares pattern.

b. $4x^2 - y^2 = (2x)^2 - y^2$ Write as $a^2 - b^2$.

$= (2x + y)(2x - y)$ Factor using difference of two squares pattern.

Exercises for Example 1

Factor the expression.

1. $16 - 9y^2$

2. $4q^2 - 49$

3. $36 - 25x^2$

Algebra 1
Practice Workbook with Examples

Practice with Examples

For use with pages 619–624

EXAMPLE 2 *Factoring Perfect Square Trinomials*

a. $x^2 - 6x + 9$

b. $9y^2 + 12y + 4$

SOLUTION

a. $x^2 - 6x + 9 = x^2 - 2(x)(3) + 3^2$ Write as $a^2 - 2ab + b^2$.

              $= (x - 3)^2$ Factor using perfect square trinomials.

b. $9y^2 + 12y + 4 = (3y)^2 + 2(3y)(2) + 2^2$ Write as $a^2 + 2ab + b^2$.

              $= (3y + 2)^2$ Factor using perfect square trinomial pattern.

Exercises for Example 2

Factor the expression.

4. $x^2 - 18x + 81$ **5.** $4n^2 + 20n + 25$ **6.** $16y^2 + 8y + 1$

EXAMPLE 3 *Solving a Quadratic Equation*

Solve the equation $2x^2 - 28x + 98 = 0$.

SOLUTION

     $2x^2 - 28x + 98 = 0$ Write original equation.

     $2(x^2 - 14x + 49) = 0$ Factor out common factor.

     $2[x^2 - 2(7x) + 7^2] = 0$ Write as $a^2 - 2ab + b^2$.

     $2(x - 7)^2 = 0$ Factor using perfect square trinomial pattern.

     $x - 7 = 0$ Set repeated factor equal to 0.

     $x = 7$ Solve for x.

The solution is 7.

Practice with Examples

For use with pages 619–624

Exercises for Example 3

Use factoring to solve the equation.

7. $x^2 - 20x + 100 = 0$ **8.** $4n^2 - 4n = -1$ **9.** $3z^2 - 24z + 48 = 0$

EXAMPLE 4 *Solving a Quadratic Equation*

Solve the equation $75 - 48x^2 = 0$.

SOLUTION

$75 - 48x^2 = 0$	Write original equation.
$3(25 - 16x^2) = 0$	Factor out common factor.
$3[5^2 - (4x)^2] = 0$	Write as $a^2 - b^2$.
$3(5 + 4x)(5 - 4x) = 0$	Factor using difference of two squares pattern.
$(5 + 4x) = 0$ or $(5 - 4x) = 0$	Use zero-product property.
$5 + 4x = 0$	Set first factor equal to 0.
$x = -\frac{5}{4}$	Solve for x.
$5 - 4x = 0$	Set second factor equal to 0.
$x = \frac{5}{4}$	Solve for x.

The solutions are $-\frac{5}{4}$ and $\frac{5}{4}$.

Exercises for Example 4

Use factoring to solve the equation.

10. $x^2 - 49 = 0$ **11.** $9y^2 - 64 = 0$ **12.** $4x^2 = 81$

Algebra 1
Practice Workbook with Examples

Practice with Examples

For use with pages 625–632

GOAL Use the distributive property to factor a polynomial and solve polynomial equations by factoring

---

VOCABULARY

A factor is **prime** if it cannot be factored using integer coefficients.

To **factor a polynomial completely,** write it as the product of monomial factors and prime factors with at least two terms.

EXAMPLE 1 *Finding the Greatest Common Factor*

Factor the greatest common factor out of $35x^3 + 45x^5$.

SOLUTION

First find the greatest common factor (GCF). It is the product of all the common factors.

$$35x^3 = 5 \cdot 7 \cdot x \cdot x \cdot x$$
$$45x^5 = 5 \cdot 9 \cdot x \cdot x \cdot x \cdot x \cdot x$$
$$\text{GCF} = 5 \cdot x \cdot x \cdot x = 5x^3$$

Use the distributive property to factor the greatest common factor out of the polynomial.

$$35x^3 + 45x^5 = 5x^3(7 + 9x^2)$$

Exercises for Example 1

Find the greatest common factor and factor it out of the expression.

1. $24y^3 + 32y$

2. $6n^8 - 18n^3$

3. $3a^2 + 30$

Practice with Examples

For use with pages 625–632

EXAMPLE 2 *Factoring Completely*

Factor $3x^4 + 30x^3 + 27x^2$ completely.

SOLUTION

$$3x^4 + 30x^3 + 27x^2 = 3x^2(x^2 + 10x + 9) \quad \text{Factor out GCF.}$$
$$= 3x^2(x + 9)(x + 1) \quad \text{Factor } x^2 + bx + c \text{ when } b \text{ and } c \text{ are positive.}$$

Exercises for Example 2

Factor the expression completely.

4. $2y^3 - 18y$ **5.** $7t^5 + 14t^4 + 7t^3$ **6.** $x^4 - 3x^3 + 2x^2$

EXAMPLE 3 *Factoring by Grouping*

Factor $x^4 - 3x^3 + 4x - 12$ completely.

SOLUTION

Sometimes you can factor polynomials that have four terms by grouping the polynomial into two groups of terms and factoring the greatest common factor out of each term.

$$x^4 - 3x^3 + 4x - 12 = (x^4 - 3x^3) + (4x - 12) \quad \text{Group terms.}$$
$$= x^3(x - 3) + 4(x - 3) \quad \text{Factor each group.}$$
$$= (x - 3)(x^3 + 4) \quad \text{Use distributive property.}$$

Exercises for Example 3

Factor the expression completely.

7. $y^3 + 3y^2 - 2y - 6$ **8.** $x^3 + 2x^2 + 5x + 10$ **9.** $d^4 - d^3 + d - 1$

Algebra 1
Practice Workbook with Examples

NAME _____ DATE _____

Practice with Examples

For use with pages 625–632

EXAMPLE 4 *Solving a Polynomial Equation*

Solve $7x^3 - 63x = 0$.

SOLUTION

$$7x^3 - 63x = 0 \qquad \text{Write original equation.}$$
$$7x(x^2 - 9) = 0 \qquad \text{Factor out GCF.}$$
$$7x(x + 3)(x - 3) = 0 \qquad \text{Factor difference of two squares.}$$

By setting each variable factor equal to zero, you find the solutions to be 0, −3, and 3.

Exercises for Example 4

Solve the equation.

10. $y^2 - 4y - 5 = 0$

11. $3w^3 - 75w = 0$

12. $2x^3 + 12x^2 + 18x = 0$

Practice with Examples

For use with pages 643–648

Chapter 11

GOAL **Solve proportions and use proportions to solve real-life problems**

VOCABULARY

A **proportion** is an equation that states that two ratios are equal. In the proportion $\dfrac{a}{b} = \dfrac{c}{d}$, the numbers a and d are the **extremes** of the proportion and the numbers b and c are the **means** of the proportion.

Properties of Proportions

Reciprocal Property

If two ratios are equal, their reciprocals are also equal.

If $\dfrac{a}{b} = \dfrac{c}{d}$, then $\dfrac{b}{a} = \dfrac{d}{c}$.

Cross Product Property

The product of the extremes equals the product of the means.

If $\dfrac{a}{b} = \dfrac{c}{d}$, then $ad = bc$.

Solving for the variable in a proportion is called **solving the proportion.** An **extraneous** solution is a trial solution that does not satisfy the original equation.

EXAMPLE 1 *Using the Cross Product Property and Checking Solutions*

Solve the proportion $\dfrac{x^2 - 4}{x + 2} = \dfrac{x - 2}{2}$.

SOLUTION

$\dfrac{x^2 - 4}{x + 2} = \dfrac{x - 2}{2}$ Write original proportion.

$2(x^2 - 4) = (x + 2)(x - 2)$ Use cross product property. $\dfrac{x^2 - 4}{x + 2} \bowtie \dfrac{x - 2}{2}$

$2x^2 - 8 = x^2 - 4$ Use distributive property and simplify.

$x^2 = 4$ Isolate variable term.

$x = \pm 2$ Take square root of each side.

The solutions appear to be $x = 2$ and $x = -2$. You must check each solution in the original proportion to eliminate possible extraneous solutions.

NAME _____ DATE _____

Practice with Examples

For use with pages 643–648

$x = 2$:

$$\frac{x^2 - 4}{x + 2} = \frac{x - 2}{2}$$

$$\frac{2^2 - 4}{2 + 2} \overset{?}{=} \frac{2 - 2}{2}$$

$$\frac{0}{4} \overset{?}{=} \frac{0}{2}$$

$$0 = 0$$

$x = -2$:

$$\frac{x^2 - 4}{x + 2} = \frac{x - 2}{2}$$

$$\frac{(-2)^2 - 4}{(-2) + 2} \overset{?}{=} \frac{(-2) - 2}{2}$$

$$\frac{0}{0} \overset{\cancel{=}}{} \frac{-4}{2}$$

You can conclude that $x = -2$ is extraneous because the check results in a false statement. The only solution is $x = 2$.

Exercises for Example 1

Solve the proportion and check for extraneous solutions.

1. $\dfrac{4}{x} = \dfrac{x}{16}$

2. $\dfrac{x + 5}{6} = \dfrac{x - 2}{4}$

3. $\dfrac{x - 1}{2} = \dfrac{x^2 - 1}{x + 1}$

Algebra 1
Practice Workbook with Examples

NAME _____ DATE _____

Practice with Examples

For use with pages 643–648

EXAMPLE 2 ## Writing and Using a Proportion

You are making a scale model of a sailboat. The boat is 20 feet long and 15 feet high. Your scale model will be 12 inches high. How long should it be?

SOLUTION

Let L represent the length of the model.

$$\frac{\text{Length of actual boat}}{\text{Height of actual boat}} = \frac{\text{Length of model}}{\text{Height of model}}$$

$$\frac{20}{15} = \frac{L}{12}$$

The solution is $L = 16$. Your scale model should be 16 inches long.

Exercise for Example 2

4. Rework Example 3 if your scale model is 18 inches high.

NAME _____ DATE _____

Practice with Examples

For use with pages 649–655

GOAL Use equations to solve percent equations and use percents in real-life problems

---

VOCABULARY

In any percent equation the **base number** is the number that you are comparing to.

EXAMPLE 1 *Number Compared to Base is Unknown*

What is 40% of 65 meters?

SOLUTION

VERBAL MODEL	$\boxed{a}$ is $\boxed{p \text{ percent}}$ of $\boxed{b}$

LABELS   Number compared to base $= a$ (meters)

                                    Percent $= 40\% = 0.40$ (no units)

                                    Base Number $= 65$ (meters)

ALGEBRAIC MODEL $a = (0.40)(65)$

                                   $a = 26$ 26 meters is 40% of 65 meters.

Exercises for Example 1

1. What is 24% of $30?

2. What is 60% of 15 miles?

Practice with Examples

Chapter 11

EXAMPLE 2 *Base Number is Unknown*

Twenty-five miles is 20% of what distance?

SOLUTION

VERBAL MODEL	$\boxed{a}$ is $\boxed{p \text{ percent}}$ of $\boxed{b}$

LABELS

Number compared to base = 25 (miles)

Percent = 20% = 0.20   (no units)

Base Number = b (miles)

ALGEBRAIC MODEL $25 = (0.20)b$

$\dfrac{25}{0.20} = 125 = b$ Twenty-five miles is 20% of 125 miles.

Exercises for Example 2

3. Sixty grams is 40% of what weight?   **4.** Fifteen yards is 30% of what distance?

EXAMPLE 3 *Percent is Unknown*

Ninety is what percent of 15?

SOLUTION

VERBAL MODEL $\boxed{a}$ is $\boxed{p \text{ percent}}$ of $\boxed{b}$

LABELS

Number compared to base = 90 (no units)

Percent = p (no units)

Base Number = 15   (no units)

ALGEBRAIC MODEL $90 = p(15)$

$\dfrac{90}{15} = p$

$6 = p$ Decimal form

$600\% = p$ Decimal form $\left(6 = \dfrac{600}{100} \right)$

Practice with Examples

For use with pages 649–655

Exercises for Example 3

5. Forty-five is what percent of 180?

6. Sixty is what percent of 15?

EXAMPLE 4 *Modeling and Using Percents*

You took a multiple-choice exam with 200 questions. You answered 80% of the questions correctly. How many questions did you answer correctly?

SOLUTION

You can solve the problem by using a proportion. Let n represent the number of correct answers.

$$\frac{\textit{Number of correct answers}}{\textit{Total number of answers}} = \frac{80}{100} \qquad \text{Write proportion.}$$

$$\frac{n}{200} = \frac{80}{100} \qquad \text{Substitute.}$$

$$100n = 200 \cdot 80 \qquad \text{Use cross products.}$$

$$n = \frac{200 \cdot 80}{100} \qquad \text{Divide by 100.}$$

$$n = 160 \qquad \text{Simplify.}$$

You answered 160 questions correctly.

Exercise for Example 4

7. Rework Example 4 if you answered 85% of the questions correctly.

NAME _____ DATE _____

Practice with Examples

For use with pages 656–662

GOAL Use direct and inverse variation and use direct and inverse variation to model real-life situations

---

VOCABULARY

The variables x and y vary **directly** if for a constant k

$\dfrac{y}{x} = k$, or $y = kx$, $k \neq 0$.

The variables x and y vary **inversely** if for a constant k

$xy = k$, or $y = \dfrac{k}{x}$, $k \neq 0$.

The number k is the **constant of variation**.

EXAMPLE 1 *Using Direct and Inverse Variation*

When x is 4, y is 6. Find an equation that relates x and y in each case.

a. x and y vary directly   **b.** x and y vary inversely

SOLUTION

a. $\dfrac{y}{x} = k$ Write variation model.

$\dfrac{6}{4} = k$ Substitute 4 for x and 6 for y.

$\dfrac{3}{2} = k$ Simplify.

An equation that relates x and y is $\dfrac{y}{x} = \dfrac{3}{2}$, or $y = \dfrac{3}{2}x$.

b. $xy = k$ Write inverse variation model.

$(4)(6) = k$ Substitute 4 for x and 6 for y.

$24 = k$ Simplify.

An equation that relates x and y is $xy = 24$, or $y = \dfrac{24}{x}$.

Practice with Examples

For use with pages 656–662

Exercises for Example 1

When *x* is 4, *y* is 5. Find an equation that relates *x* and *y* in each case.

1. *x* and *y* vary directly

2. *x* and *y* vary inversely

EXAMPLE 2   *Writing and Using a Model*

The graph at the right shows a model for the relationship between the length of a particular rectangle and the width of the rectangle if the area of the rectangle is fixed. For the values shown, the length *l* and the width *w* vary inversely.

a. Find an inverse variation model that relates *l* and *w*.

b. Use the model to find the length for a width of 8 inches.

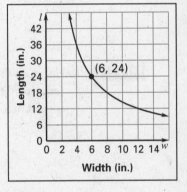

SOLUTION

a. From the graph, you can see that $l = 24$ inches when $w = 6$ inches.

$$l = \frac{k}{w}$$ Write inverse variation model.

$$24 = \frac{k}{6}$$ Substitute 24 for *l* and 6 for *w*.

$$144 = k$$ Solve for *k*.

The model is $l = \dfrac{144}{w}$, where *l* and *w* are in inches.

b. When $w = 8$ inches, $l = \dfrac{144}{8} = 18$ inches.

NAME _____ DATE _____

Practice with Examples

For use with pages 656–662

Exercises for Example 2

3. Use the model in Example 3 to find the length for a width of 4 inches.

4. Suppose the length and width of a rectangle vary inversely. When the length is 16 inches, the width is 8 inches. Find an inverse variation model that relates the length and width.

5. Using your answer to Exercise 4, find the length of the rectangle when the width is 2, 4, 16, and 20 inches.

Algebra 1
Practice Workbook with Examples

Practice with Examples

For use with pages 664–669

GOAL **Simplify a rational expression and use rational expressions to find geometric probability**

VOCABULARY

A **rational expression** is a fraction whose numerator and denominator are nonzero polynomials.

A rational expression is **simplified** if its numerator and denominator have no factors in common (other than ± 1).

EXAMPLE 1 *Simplifying a Rational Expression*

Simplify the expression if possible.

a. $\dfrac{x^2 - 5}{x}$ b. $\dfrac{x^2 - 6x}{3x^2}$

SOLUTION

a. When you simplify rational expressions, you can divide out only factors, not terms. You cannot simplify $\dfrac{x^2 - 5}{x}$. You cannot divide out the common term x.

b. $\dfrac{x^2 - 6x}{3x^2} = \dfrac{\cancel{x}(x - 6)}{\cancel{x} \cdot 3x}$ You can divide out the common factor x.

$\phantom{\dfrac{x^2 - 6x}{3x^2}} = \dfrac{x - 6}{3x}$ Simplified form

Exercises for Example 1

Simplify the expression if possible.

1. $\dfrac{3x}{4x + x^2}$

2. $\dfrac{x^2(x - 7)}{x^3}$

3. $\dfrac{x^3 + 3}{x^3}$

NAME _____ DATE _____

Practice with Examples

For use with pages 664–669

EXAMPLE 2 *Recognizing Opposite Factors*

Simplify $\dfrac{x^2 - 6x + 8}{4 - x}$.

SOLUTION

$$\frac{x^2 - 6x + 8}{4 - x} = \frac{(x - 2)(x - 4)}{4 - x} \qquad \text{Factor numerator and denominator.}$$

$$= \frac{(x - 2)(x - 4)}{-(x - 4)} \qquad \text{Factor } -1 \text{ out of denominator.}$$

$$= \frac{(x - 2)(x - 4)}{-(x - 4)} \qquad \text{Divide out common factor } x - 4.$$

$$= -(x - 2) \qquad \text{Simplified form}$$

Exercises for Example 2

Simplify the expression of possible.

4. $\dfrac{x^2 - 8x + 12}{2 - x}$

5. $\dfrac{1 - x^2}{x^2 - 3x + 2}$

6. $\dfrac{1 - x}{x^2 + 2x - 3}$

Algebra 1
Practice Workbook with Examples

Chapter 11

NAME _____ DATE _____

Practice with Examples

For use with pages 664–669

EXAMPLE 3 *Writing and Using a Rational Model*

A coin is tossed into the large rectangle region shown at the right. It is equally likely to land on any point in the region. Write a model that gives the probability that the coin will land in the small rectangle.

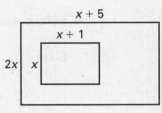

SOLUTION

$$P = \frac{\text{Area of small rectangle}}{\text{Area of large rectangle}}$$ Formula for geometric probability

$$= \frac{x(x + 1)}{2x(x + 5)}$$ Find areas.

$$= \frac{\cancel{x}(x + 1)}{2\cancel{x}(x + 5)}$$ Divide out common factors.

$$= \frac{x + 1}{2(x + 5)}$$ Simplify.

Exercise for Example 3

7. Rework Example 3 if the area of the small rectangle is $x(x + 2)$.

Chapter 11

NAME _____ DATE _____

Practice with Examples

For use with pages 670–675

GOAL **Multiply and divide rational expressions and use rational expressions as real-life models**

VOCABULARY

Let a, b, c, and d be nonzero numbers.

To multiply rational expressions, multiply numerators and denominators.

$$\frac{a}{b} \cdot \frac{c}{d} = \frac{ac}{bd}$$

To divide rational expressions, multiply by the reciprocal of the divisor.

$$\frac{a}{b} \div \frac{c}{d} = \frac{a}{b} \cdot \frac{d}{c}$$

EXAMPLE 1 **Multiplying Rational Expressions Involving Polynomials**

Simplify $\dfrac{x + 3}{x^2 - 4} \cdot \dfrac{x + 2}{x^2 + 4x + 3}$.

SOLUTION

$$\frac{x + 3}{x^2 - 4} \cdot \frac{x + 2}{x^2 + 4x + 3} = \frac{(x + 3)(x + 2)}{(x^2 - 4)(x^2 + 4x + 3)}$$

    Multiply numerators and denominators.

$$= \frac{(x + 3)(x + 2)}{(x + 2)(x - 2)(x + 3)(x + 1)}$$

    Factor and divide out common factors.

$$= \frac{1}{(x - 2)(x + 1)}$$

    Simplified form

NAME _____ DATE _____

Practice with Examples

For use with pages 670–675

Exercises for Example 1

Simplify the expression.

1. $\dfrac{5x}{x^2 - 2x - 8} \cdot \dfrac{2x - 8}{5x^2}$

2. $\dfrac{x^2 - 9}{6} \cdot \dfrac{3x + 6}{x^2 - x - 6}$

EXAMPLE 2 *Dividing by a Polynomial*

Simplify $\dfrac{x^2 - x - 12}{x^2 - 9} \div (x - 4)$.

SOLUTION

$\dfrac{x^2 - x - 12}{x^2 - 9} \div (x - 4) = \dfrac{x^2 - x - 12}{x^2 - 9} \cdot \dfrac{1}{x - 4}$ Multiply by reciprocal.

$= \dfrac{x^2 - x - 12}{(x^2 - 9)(x - 4)}$ Multiply numerators and denominators.

$= \dfrac{(x - 4)(x + 3)}{(x + 3)(x - 3)(x - 4)}$ Divide out common factors.

$= \dfrac{1}{x - 3}$ Simplified form

NAME _____ DATE _____

Practice with Examples

For use with pages 670–675

Exercises for Example 2

Simplify the expression.

3. $\dfrac{x^2 - 49}{x} \div 5(x + 7)$

4. $\dfrac{x^2 - 5x + 4}{x^2} \div (x - 1)$

Practice with Examples

For use with pages 676–682

GOAL   Add and subtract rational expressions that have like denominators and add and subtract rational expressions that have unlike denominators

---

VOCABULARY

Let a, b, and c be any real numbers, with $c \neq 0$.

To **add,** add the numerators. $\dfrac{a}{c} + \dfrac{b}{c} = \dfrac{a + b}{c}$

To **subtract,** subtract the numerators. $\dfrac{a}{c} - \dfrac{b}{c} = \dfrac{a - b}{c}$

The least common multiple of unlike denominators is called the **least common denominator,** or LCD.

EXAMPLE 1   *Simplifying after Subtracting Expressions with Like Denominators*

Simplify $\dfrac{5x}{2x^2 + x - 1} - \dfrac{3x + 1}{2x^2 + x - 1}$.

SOLUTION

$$\frac{5x}{2x^2 + x - 1} - \frac{3x + 1}{2x^2 + x - 1} = \frac{5x - (3x + 1)}{2x^2 + x - 1} \qquad \text{Subtract.}$$

$$= \frac{2x - 1}{2x^2 + x - 1} \qquad \text{Simplify.}$$

$$= \frac{2x - 1}{(2x - 1)(x + 1)} \qquad \text{Divide out common factor.}$$

$$= \frac{1}{x + 1} \qquad \text{Simplified form}$$

Exercises for Example 1

Simplify the expression.

1. $\dfrac{2x}{x^2 + 5x + 6} - \dfrac{x - 2}{x^2 + 5x + 6}$

2. $\dfrac{x}{x^2 - 16} - \dfrac{4}{x^2 - 16}$

Practice with Examples

For use with pages 676–682

EXAMPLE 2 **Adding Expressions with Unlike Denominators**

Simplify $\dfrac{3}{4x} + \dfrac{5}{6x^2}$.

SOLUTION

The LCD contains the highest power of each factor that appears in either denominator, so the LCD is $2^2 \cdot 3 \cdot x^2$, or $12x^2$.

$$\frac{3}{4x} + \frac{5}{6x^2} = \frac{3 \cdot 3x}{4x \cdot 3x} + \frac{5 \cdot 2}{6x^2 \cdot 2} \quad \text{Rewrite fractions using LCD.}$$

$$= \frac{9x}{12x^2} + \frac{10}{12x^2} \quad \text{Simplify numerator and denominator.}$$

$$= \frac{9x + 10}{12x^2} \quad \text{Add fractions.}$$

Exercises for Example 2

Simplify the expression.

3. $\dfrac{3}{5x} + \dfrac{2}{7x}$

4. $\dfrac{4}{x + 1} + \dfrac{5}{x + 2}$

5. $\dfrac{3x}{x + 4} + \dfrac{1}{2x + 8}$

NAME _____ DATE _____

Practice with Examples

For use with pages 676–682

EXAMPLE 3 *Subtracting Expressions with Unlike Denominators*

Simplify $\dfrac{x}{x + 2} - \dfrac{3}{x - 3}$.

SOLUTION

The least common denominator is the product $(x + 2)(x - 3)$.

$$\frac{x}{x + 2} - \frac{3}{x - 3} = \frac{x(x - 3)}{(x + 2)(x - 3)} - \frac{3(x + 2)}{(x + 2)(x - 3)} \qquad \text{Rewrite fractions using LCD.}$$

$$= \frac{x^2 - 3x}{(x + 2)(x - 3)} - \frac{3x + 6}{(x + 2)(x - 3)} \qquad \text{Simplify numerators. Leave denominators in factored form.}$$

$$= \frac{x^2 - 3x - (3x + 6)}{(x + 2)(x - 3)} \qquad \text{Subtract fractions.}$$

$$= \frac{x^2 - 3x - 3x - 6}{(x + 2)(x - 3)} \qquad \text{Use the distributive property.}$$

$$= \frac{x^2 - 6x - 6}{(x + 2)(x - 3)} \qquad \text{Simplified form}$$

Exercises for Example 3

Simplify the expression.

6. $\dfrac{x + 1}{x^2} - \dfrac{2}{3x}$

7. $\dfrac{2}{x + 1} - \dfrac{3}{x + 3}$

8. $\dfrac{3x}{x^2 + 2x} - \dfrac{4}{x + 2}$

Practice with Examples

For use with pages 684–689

GOAL Divide a polynomial by a monomial or by a binomial factor and use polynomial long division

EXAMPLE 1 *Dividing a Polynomial by a Monomial*

Divide $35x^3 - 45x^2 - 15x$ by $5x^2$.

SOLUTION

$$\frac{35x^3 - 45x^2 - 15x}{5x^2} = \frac{35x^3}{5x^2} - \frac{45x^2}{5x^2} - \frac{15x}{5x^2} \qquad \text{Divide each term of numerator by } 5x^2.$$

$$= \frac{7x(5x^2)}{5x^2} - \frac{9(5x^2)}{5x^2} - \frac{3(5x)}{5x^2} \qquad \text{Find common factors.}$$

$$= \frac{7x(5\cancel{x^2})}{5\cancel{x^2}} - \frac{9(5\cancel{x^2})}{5\cancel{x^2}} - \frac{3(5\cancel{x})}{5\cancel{x} \cdot x} \qquad \text{Divide out common factors.}$$

$$= 7x - 9 - \frac{3}{x} \qquad \text{Simplified form}$$

Exercises for Example 1

1. Divide $42y^2 + 24y - 30$ by $6y$.

2. Divide $-18x^2 + 21x$ by $-3x$.

Algebra 1
Practice Workbook with Examples

NAME _____ DATE _____

Practice with Examples

For use with pages 684–689

EXAMPLE 2 **Polynomial Long Division**

Divide $x^2 + 7x + 5$ by $x + 3$.

SOLUTION

$$\begin{array}{r} x + 4 \\ x + 3 \overline{)\, x^2 + 7x + 5} \\ \underline{x^2 + 3x} \\ 4x + 5 \\ \underline{4x + 12} \\ -7 \end{array}$$

1. Think: $(x^2) \div x = x$
2. Subtract $x(x + 3)$.
3. Bring down $+5$. Think: $(4x) \div x = 4$
4. Subtract $4(x + 3)$.
5. Remainder is -7.

Quotient

Dividend $\longrightarrow$ $\dfrac{x^2 + 7x + 5}{x + 3} = x + 4 + \dfrac{-7}{x + 3}$ $\longleftarrow$ Remainder
Divisor $\longrightarrow$

The answer is $x + 4 + \dfrac{-7}{x + 3}$.

Exercises for Example 2

3. Divide $x^2 - 4x - 6$ by $x + 1$.

4. Divide $x^2 + 6x - 12$ by $x - 3$.

5. Divide $3x^2 - 5x - 10$ by $3x - 2$.

6. Divide $2x^2 + 5x + 3$ by $2x - 1$.

7. Divide $4x^2 + x - 13$ by $x + 8$.

8. Divide $-6x^2 + 15x - 1$ by $x - 5$.

NAME _____ DATE _____

Practice with Examples

For use with pages 684–689

EXAMPLE 3 *Rewriting in Standard Form and Adding a Place-holding Zero*

Divide $2x^2 - 30$ by $3 + x$.

SOLUTION

First write the divisor $3 + x$ in standard form as $x + 3$. Then insert a place-holding term $0x$ in the dividend: $2x^2 - 30 = 2x^2 + 0x - 30$.

1. Think: $(2x^2) \div x = 2x$

$$
\begin{array}{r}
2x - 6 \\
x + 3 \overline{\smash{)}\ 2x^2 + 0x - 30} \\
\underline{2x^2 + 6x} \\
-6x - 30 \\
\underline{-6x - 18} \\
-12
\end{array}
$$

2. Subtract $(2x)(x + 3)$.
3. Bring down -30. Think: $(-6x) \div (x) = -6$
4. Subtract $-6(x + 3)$.
5. Remainder is -12.

The answer is $2x - 6 + \dfrac{-12}{x + 3}$.

Exercises for Example 3

9. Divide $4x^2 - 1$ by $x - 3$.

10. Divide $6y^2 + 3y - 15$ by $2 + y$.

11. Divide $6x^2 - 3$ by $x - 1$.

12. Divide $4x^2 + 10x - 7$ by $4 + x$.

Practice with Examples

For use with pages 690–697

GOAL **Solve rational equations and graph rational equations**

> **VOCABULARY**
>
> A **rational equation** is an equation that contains rational expressions.
>
> A **rational function** is a function of the form $f(x) = \dfrac{\text{polynomial}}{\text{polynomial}}$.
>
> The graph of the rational function $y = \dfrac{a}{x - h} + k$ is a **hyperbola** whose **center** is (h, k).
>
> The vertical and horizontal lines through the center are the *asymptotes* of the hyperbola.
>
> An **asymptote** is a line that a graph approaches more and more closely; however, the asymptote is not part of the graph.

EXAMPLE 1 *Cross Multiplying*

Solve $\dfrac{2}{x} = \dfrac{x + 2}{4}$.

SOLUTION

$\dfrac{2}{x} = \dfrac{x + 2}{4}$ Write original equation.

$2(4) = x(x + 2)$ Cross multiply.

$8 = x^2 + 2x$ Simplify.

$0 = x^2 + 2x - 8$ Write in standard form.

$0 = (x + 4)(x - 2)$ Factor right side.

If you set each factor equal to 0, the solutions are -4 and 2.

Exercises for Example 1

Solve the equation by cross multiplying.

1. $\dfrac{5}{w - 3} = \dfrac{w}{2}$

2. $\dfrac{6}{x + 1} = \dfrac{4}{x + 2}$

3. $\dfrac{t}{9} = \dfrac{2}{t - 3}$

Practice with Examples

For use with pages 690–697

EXAMPLE 2 *Factoring to Find the LCD*

Solve $\dfrac{1}{x - 2} + 1 = \dfrac{8}{x^2 - 5x + 6}$.

SOLUTION

The denominator $x^2 - 5x + 6$ factors as $(x - 2)(x - 3)$, so the LCD is $(x - 2)(x - 3)$. Multiply each side of the equation by $(x - 2)(x - 3)$.

$$\frac{1}{x - 2} \cdot (x - 2)(x - 3) + 1 \cdot (x - 2)(x - 3) = \frac{8}{x^2 - 5x + 6} \cdot (x - 2)(x - 3)$$

$$\frac{1(x - 2)(x - 3)}{x - 2} + (x - 2)(x - 3) = \frac{8(x - 2)(x - 3)}{(x - 2)(x - 3)}$$

$$x - 3 + x^2 - 5x + 6 = 8$$

$$x^2 - 4x + 3 = 8$$

$$x^2 - 4x - 5 = 0$$

$$(x - 5)(x + 1) = 0$$

The solutions are 5 and -1.

Exercises for Example 2

Solve the equation by multiplying by the least common denominator.

4. $\dfrac{1}{2x - 10} - \dfrac{2}{x - 5} = \dfrac{3}{4}$

5. $\dfrac{11}{x^2 - 16} = \dfrac{x}{x + 4} - 2$

NAME _____ DATE _____

Practice with Examples

For use with pages 690–697

EXAMPLE 3 *Graphing a Rational Function*

Sketch the graph of $y = \dfrac{1}{x + 1} + 3$.

SOLUTION

The graph of the rational function $y = \dfrac{a}{x - h} + k$ is a hyperbola whose center is (h, k). For the function $y = \dfrac{1}{x + 1} + 3$, the center is $(-1, 3)$. The asymptotes can be drawn as dashed lines through the center. Make a table of values and plot the points. Connect the points with two smooth branches.

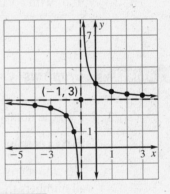

x	−4	−3	−2	−1.5	−1	0	1	2	3
y	2.$\overline{6}$	2.5	2	1	undefined	4	3.5	3.$\overline{3}$	3.25

Exercises for Example 3

6. Sketch the graph of $y = \dfrac{1}{x} + 3$.

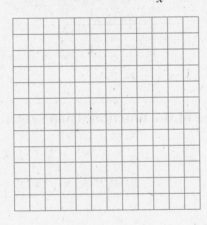

7. Sketch the graph of $y = \dfrac{4}{x - 3} - 5$.

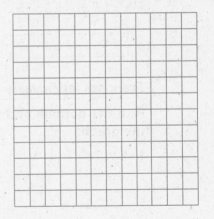

Chapter 11

Practice with Examples

For use with pages 709–714

GOAL Evaluate and graph a square-root function and use square-root functions to model real-life problems

> ### VOCABULARY
>
> A **square-root function** is a function whose equation contains a square root with a variable in the radicand.

EXAMPLE 1 *Graphing* $y = a\sqrt{x} + k$

Find the domain and the range of $y = 3\sqrt{x} + 2$. Then sketch its graph.

SOLUTION

The domain is the set of all nonnegative numbers. The range is the set of all numbers that are greater than or equal to 2. Make a table of values, plot the points, and connect them with a smooth curve.

x	y
0	$y = 3\sqrt{0} + 2 = 2$
1	$y = 3\sqrt{1} + 2 = 5$
2	$y = 3\sqrt{2} + 2 \approx 6.2$
3	$y = 3\sqrt{3} + 2 \approx 7.2$
4	$y = 3\sqrt{4} + 2 = 8$

(Graph showing the curve $y = 3\sqrt{x} + 2$ passing through points (0, 2), (1, 5), and (4, 8).)

Exercises for Example 1

Find the domain and the range of the function. Then sketch the graph.

1. $y = 2\sqrt{x} + 1$

2. $y = 2\sqrt{x} - 1$

3. $y = 2\sqrt{x} - 2$

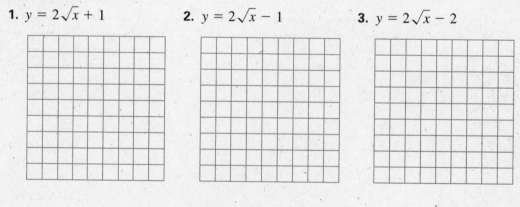

Algebra 1
Practice Workbook with Examples

Practice with Examples

For use with pages 709–714

EXAMPLE 2   *Graphing* $y = \sqrt{x - h}$

Find the domain and the range of $y = \sqrt{x - 2}$. Then sketch its graph.

SOLUTION

To find the domain, find the values of x for which the radicand is nonnegative.

$x - 2 \geq 0$ Write an inequality for the domain.

$x \geq 2$ Add two to each side.

The domain is the set of all numbers that are greater than or equal to 2. The range is the set of all nonnegative numbers. Make a table of values, plot the points, and connect them with a smooth curve.

x	y
2	$y = \sqrt{2 - 2} = 0$
3	$y = \sqrt{3 - 2} = 1$
4	$y = \sqrt{4 - 2} \approx 1.4$
5	$y = \sqrt{5 - 2} \approx 1.7$
6	$y = \sqrt{6 - 2} = 2$

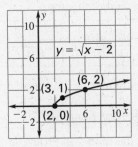

Exercises for Example 2

Find the domain and the range of the function. Then sketch its graph.

4. $y = \sqrt{x - 1}$ **5.** $y = \sqrt{x + 1}$ **6.** $y = \sqrt{x - 4}$

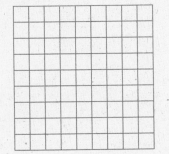

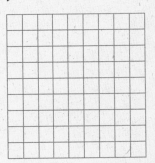

Algebra 1
Practice Workbook with Examples

Chapter 12

NAME _____ DATE _____

Practice with Examples

For use with pages 709-714

EXAMPLE 3 *Using a Square-Root Model*

An object has been dropped from a height of h feet. The speed S (in ft/sec) of the object right before it strikes the ground is given by the model $S = \sqrt{64h}$.

a. Sketch the graph of the model.

b. Find the speed S (in ft/sec) of an object that has been dropped from a height of 25 feet.

Falling Object

SOLUTION

a. Make a table of values, plot the points, and connect them with a smooth curve.

h	0	1	2	3	4
S	$\sqrt{64 \cdot 0} = 0$	$\sqrt{64 \cdot 1} = 8$	$\sqrt{64 \cdot 2} \approx 11.3$	$\sqrt{64 \cdot 3} \approx 13.9$	$\sqrt{64 \cdot 4} = 16$

b. Substitute $h = 25$ into the model: $S = \sqrt{64 \cdot 25} = 40$ ft/sec

Exercise for Example 3

7. Use the model in Example 3 to find the speed S (in ft/sec) of an object that has been dropped from a height of 36 feet.

Algebra 1
Practice Workbook with Examples

NAME _____ DATE _____

Practice with Examples

For use with pages 716–721

GOAL Add, subtract, multiply, and divide radical expressions and use radical expressions in real-life situations

VOCABULARY

Two radical expressions are **like radicals** if they have the same radicand. The expressions $\left(a + \sqrt{b}\right)$ and $\left(a - \sqrt{b}\right)$ are **conjugates** of each other.

EXAMPLE 1 *Adding and Subtracting Radicals*

Simplify the expression
$\sqrt{12} + \sqrt{3}$.

SOLUTION

$$\sqrt{12} + \sqrt{3} = \sqrt{4 \cdot 3} + \sqrt{3} \qquad \text{Perfect square factor}$$
$$= \sqrt{4} \cdot \sqrt{3} + \sqrt{3} \qquad \text{Use product property.}$$
$$= 2\sqrt{3} + \sqrt{3} \qquad \text{Simplify.}$$
$$= 3\sqrt{3} \qquad \text{Add like radicals.}$$

Exercises for Example 1

Simplify the expression.

1. $\sqrt{7} + 3\sqrt{7}$

2. $\sqrt{8} - \sqrt{2}$

3. $\sqrt{48} + \sqrt{3}$

Practice with Examples

For use with pages 716–721

EXAMPLE 2 *Multiplying Radicals*

Simplify the expression.

a. $\sqrt{3} \cdot \sqrt{12}$ **b.** $\sqrt{5}(\sqrt{2} + \sqrt{3})$ **c.** $(3 + \sqrt{2})(3 - \sqrt{2})$

SOLUTION

a. $\sqrt{3} \cdot \sqrt{12} = \sqrt{36}$ Use product property.

$= 6$ Simplify.

b. $\sqrt{5}(\sqrt{2} + \sqrt{3}) = \sqrt{5} \cdot \sqrt{2} + \sqrt{5} \cdot \sqrt{3}$ Use distributive property.

$= \sqrt{10} + \sqrt{15}$ Use product property.

c. $(3 + \sqrt{2})(3 - \sqrt{2}) = 3^2 - (\sqrt{2})^2$ Use sum and difference pattern.

$= 9 - 2 = 7$ Simplify.

Exercises for Example 2

Simplify the expression.

4. $(\sqrt{2} + 1)^2$ **5.** $\sqrt{3} \cdot \sqrt{6}$ **6.** $\sqrt{10}(2 + \sqrt{2})$

EXAMPLE 3 *Simplifying Radicals*

Simplify $\dfrac{5}{\sqrt{2}}$.

SOLUTION

$$\frac{5}{\sqrt{2}} = \frac{5}{\sqrt{2}} \cdot \frac{\sqrt{2}}{\sqrt{2}}$$ Multiply numerator and denominator by $\sqrt{2}$.

$$= \frac{5\sqrt{2}}{\sqrt{2} \cdot \sqrt{2}}$$ Multiply fractions.

$$= \frac{5\sqrt{2}}{2}$$ Simplify.

Algebra 1
Practice Workbook with Examples

NAME _____ DATE _____

Practice with Examples

For use with pages 716–721

Exercises for Example 3

Simplify the expression.

7. $\dfrac{4}{\sqrt{3}}$

8. $\dfrac{5}{\sqrt{8}}$

9. $\dfrac{-1}{\sqrt{12}}$

EXAMPLE 4 *Using a Radical Model*

A tsunami is an enormous ocean wave that can be caused by underwater earthquakes, volcanic eruptions, or hurricanes. The speed S of a tsunami in miles per hour is given by the model $S = 3.86\sqrt{d}$ where d is the depth of the ocean in feet. Suppose one tsunami is at a depth of 1792 feet and another is at a depth of 1372 feet. Write an expression that represents the difference in speed between the tsunamis. Simplify the expression.

SOLUTION

The speed of the first tsunami mentioned is $3.86\sqrt{1792}$ while the speed of the second tsunami is $3.86\sqrt{1372}$. The difference D between the speeds can be represented by $3.86\sqrt{1792} - 3.86\sqrt{1372}$.

$$
\begin{aligned}
D &= 3.86\sqrt{1792} - 3.86\sqrt{1372} \\
  &= 3.86\sqrt{7 \cdot 256} - 3.86\sqrt{7 \cdot 196} \\
  &= 61.76\sqrt{7} - 54.04\sqrt{7} = 7.72\sqrt{7}
\end{aligned}
$$

Exercise for Example 4

10. Rework Example 4 if one tsunami is at a depth of 3125 feet and another tsunami is at a depth of 2000 feet.

Chapter 12

Practice with Examples

For use with pages 722–728

GOAL Solve a radical equation and use radical equations to solve real-life problems

EXAMPLE 1 *Solving a Radical Equation*

Solve $\sqrt{3x + 1} + 2 = 6$.

SOLUTION

Isolate the radical expression on one side of the equation.

$\sqrt{3x + 1} + 2 = 6$	Write original equation.
$\sqrt{3x + 1} = 4$	Subtract 2 from each side.
$(\sqrt{3x + 1})^2 = 4^2$	Square each side.
$3x + 1 = 16$	Simplify.
$3x = 15$	Subtract 1 from each side.
$x = 5$	Divide each side by 3.

The solution is 5.

Exercises for Example 1

Solve the equation.

1. $\sqrt{x + 2} = 3$

2. $\sqrt{x} + 2 = 3$

3. $\sqrt{4x + 1} = 3$

Algebra 1
Practice Workbook with Examples

NAME _____ DATE _____

Practice with Examples

For use with pages 722–728

EXAMPLE 2 *Checking for Extraneous Solutions*

Solve the equation $\sqrt{2x + 3} = x$.

SOLUTION

$\sqrt{2x + 3} = x$	Write original equation.
$(\sqrt{2x + 3})^2 = x^2$	Square each side.
$2x + 3 = x^2$	Simplify.
$0 = x^2 - 2x - 3$	Write in standard form.
$0 = (x - 3)(x + 1)$	Factor.
$x = 3 \text{ or } x = -1$	Zero-product property.

To check the solutions, substitute 3 and -1 in the original equation.

$$\sqrt{2(3) + 3} \stackrel{?}{=} 3 \qquad\qquad \sqrt{2(-1) + 3} \stackrel{?}{=} -1$$
$$\sqrt{9} \stackrel{?}{=} 3 \qquad\qquad\qquad \sqrt{1} \stackrel{?}{=} -1$$
$$3 = 3 \qquad\qquad\qquad\qquad 1 \neq -1$$

The only solution is 3, because $x = -1$ is not a solution.

Exercises for Example 2

Solve the equation and check for extraneous solutions.

4. $\sqrt{x - 1} + 3 = x$

5. $\sqrt{3x} + 6 = 0$

6. $\sqrt{x + 6} = x$

NAME _____ DATE _____

Practice with Examples

For use with pages 722–728

EXAMPLE 3 *Using a Radical Model*

The distance d (in centimeters) that tap water is absorbed up a strip of blotting paper at a temperature of 28.4°C is given by the model

$d = 0.444\sqrt{t}$ where t is the time (in seconds).

Approximately how many minutes would it take for the water to travel a distance of 16 centimeters up the strip of blotting paper?

SOLUTION

$d = 0.444\sqrt{t}$	Write model for blotting paper distance.
$16 = 0.444\sqrt{t}$	Substitute 16 for d.
$\dfrac{16}{0.444} = \sqrt{t}$	Divide each side by 0.444.
$\left(\dfrac{16}{0.444}\right)^2 = t$	Square each side.
$1299 \approx t$	Use a calculator.

It would take approximately 1299 seconds for the water to travel a distance of 16 centimeters up the strip of blotting paper. To find the time in minutes, you divide 1299 by 60. It would take approximately 22 minutes.

Exercises for Example 3

7. Use the model in Example 3 to find the distance that the water would travel in 36 seconds.

8. Use the model in Example 3 to find the number of seconds that it would take for the water to travel a distance of 10 centimeters up the strip of blotting paper.

Chapter 12

Practice with Examples

For use with pages 730–736

GOAL Solve a quadratic equation by completing the square and choose a method for solving a quadratic equation

---

VOCABULARY

To complete the square of the expression $x^2 + bx$, add the square of half the coefficient of x.

$$x^2 + bx + \left(\frac{b}{2}\right)^2 = \left(x + \frac{b}{2}\right)^2$$

EXAMPLE 1 *The Leading Coefficient is Not 1*

Solve $9x^2 - 18x + 5 = 0$ by completing the square.

SOLUTION

When the quadratic equation's leading coefficient is not 1, divide each side of the equation by this coefficient *before* completing the square.

$9x^2 - 18x + 5 = 0$	Write original equation.
$9x^2 - 18x = -5$	Subtract 5 from each side.
$x^2 - 2x = -\dfrac{5}{9}$	Divide each side by 9.
$x^2 - 2x + \left(\dfrac{2}{2}\right)^2 = -\dfrac{5}{9} + 1$	Add $\left(\dfrac{2}{2}\right)^2$, or 1 to each side.
$(x - 1)^2 = \dfrac{4}{9}$	Write left side as perfect square.
$(x - 1) = \pm\dfrac{2}{3}$	Find square root of each side.
$x = 1 \pm \dfrac{2}{3}$	Add 1 to each side.

The solutions are $\dfrac{5}{3}$ and $\dfrac{1}{3}$. Both solutions check in the original equation.

Chapter 12

Algebra 1
Practice Workbook with Examples

Practice with Examples

For use with pages 730–736

Exercises for Example 1

Solve the equation by completing the square.

1. $2n^2 - 3n = 2$ **2.** $3y^2 + 4y = -1$ **3.** $4b^2 + 8b + 3 = 0$

EXAMPLE 2 *Choosing a Solution Method*

Choose a method to solve the quadratic equation.

    a. $5x^2 + 3x - 2 = 0$ **b.** $x^2 + 6x - 1 = 0$

SOLUTION

    a. This equation can be factored easily.

$5x^2 + 3x - 2 = 0$	Write original equation.
$(5x - 2)(x + 1) = 0$	Factor.
$5x - 2 = 0$ or $x + 1 = 0$	Zero-product property.
$x = \dfrac{2}{5}$ or $x = -1$	Solve for x.

The solutions are $\dfrac{2}{5}$ and -1.

    b. When this equation is written as $ax^2 + bx + c = 0$, $a = 1$ and b is an even number. Therefore it can be solved by completing the square.

$x^2 + 6x - 1 = 0$	Write original equation.
$x^2 + 6x = 1$	Add 1 to each side.
$x^2 + 6x + \left(\dfrac{6}{2}\right)^2 = 1 + 9$	Add $\left(\dfrac{6}{2}\right)^2$, or 9 to each side.
$(x + 3)^2 = 10$	Write left side as perfect square.
$x + 3 = \pm\sqrt{10}$	Find square root of each side.
$x = -3 \pm \sqrt{10}$	Subtract 3 from each side.

The solutions are $-3 + \sqrt{10}$ and $-3 - \sqrt{10}$.

Algebra 1
Practice Workbook with Examples

NAME _____ DATE _____

Practice with Examples

For use with pages 730–736

Exercises for Example 2

Choose a method to solve the quadratic equation. Explain your choice.

4. $5y^2 - 35 = 0$

5. $w^2 - 3w - 10 = 0$

6. $2.7x^2 + 0.5x - 7 = 0$

Chapter 12

NAME _____ DATE _____

Practice with Examples

For use with pages 738–744

GOAL Use the Pythagorean theorem and its converse and use the Pythagorean theorem in real-life problems

---

VOCABULARY

In a right trangle, the **hypotenuse** is the side opposite the right angle; the other two sides are the **legs**.

The **Pythagorean theorem** states that if a triangle is a right triangle, then the sum of the squares of the lengths of the legs a and b equals the square of the length of the hypotenuse c, or $a^2 + b^2 = c^2$.

In a statement of the form "If p, then q," p is the **hypothesis** and q is the **conclusion.** The **converse** of the statement "If p, then q" is the related statement "If q, then p."

The **converse of the Pythagorean theorem** states that if a triangle has side lengths a, b, and c such that $a^2 + b^2 = c^2$, then the triangle is a right triangle.

EXAMPLE 1 *Using the Pythagorean Theorem*

A right triangle has one leg that is 1 inch longer than the other leg. The hypotenuse is 5 inches. Find the lengths of the legs.

SOLUTION

Sketch a right triangle and label the sides. Let x be the length of the shorter leg. Use the Pythagorean theorem to solve for x.

$$a^2 + b^2 = c^2 \qquad \text{Write Pythagorean theorem.}$$
$$x^2 + (x + 1)^2 = 5^2 \qquad \text{Substitute for } a, b, \text{ and } c.$$
$$x^2 + x^2 + 2x + 1 = 25 \qquad \text{Simplify.}$$
$$2x^2 + 2x - 24 = 0 \qquad \text{Write in standard form.}$$
$$2(x + 4)(x - 3) = 0 \qquad \text{Factor.}$$
$$x = -4 \text{ or } x = 3 \qquad \text{Zero-product property.}$$

Distance is positive. The sides have lengths 3 inches and $3 + 1 = 4$ inches.

Practice with Examples

For use with pages 738–744

Exercises for Example 1

Use the Pythagorean theorem to find the missing length of the right triangle.

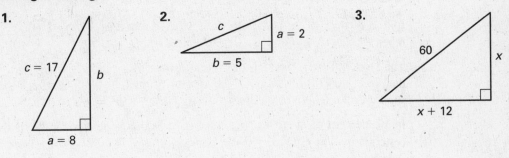

1.

$c = 17$
b
$a = 8$

2.

c
$a = 2$
$b = 5$

3.

60
x
$x + 12$

EXAMPLE 2 *Determining Right Triangles*

Determine whether the given lengths are sides of a right triangle.

a. 2.5, 6, 6.5   **b.** 10, 24, 25

SOLUTION

Use the converse of the Pythagorean theorem.

a. The lengths are sides of a right triangle because

$$2.5^2 + 6^2 = 6.25 + 36 = 42.25 = 6.5^2.$$

b. The lengths are not sides of a right triangle because

$$10^2 + 24^2 = 100 + 576 = 676 \neq 25^2.$$

Chapter 12

NAME _____ DATE _____

Practice with Examples

For use with pages 738–744

Exercises for Example 2

Determine whether the given lengths are sides of a right triangle.

4. 8, 15, 17

5. 3, 6, 7

6. 9, 40, 41

Chapter 12

Practice with Examples

For use with pages 745–750

GOAL **Find the distance between two points in a coordinate plane and find the midpoint between two points in a coordinate plane**

> ### VOCABULARY
>
> The **midpoint** between two points is the point that lies on the line connecting the two points and is halfway between the two points.

EXAMPLE 1 *Finding the Distance Between Two Points*

Find the distance between $(-1, 2)$ and $(3, 7)$ using the distance formula.

$$d = \sqrt{(x_2 - x_1)^2 + (y_2 - y_1)^2}$$ Write distance formula.

$$= \sqrt{(-1 - 3)^2 + (2 - 7)^2}$$ Substitute.

$$= \sqrt{41}$$ Simplify.

$$\approx 6.40$$ Use a calculator.

Exercises for Example 1

Find the distance between the two points. Round the result to the nearest hundredth if necessary.

1. $(0, 4), (-3, 0)$

2. $(2, 3), (4, 5)$

3. $(-4, 2), (1, 4)$

Algebra 1
Practice Workbook with Examples

Chapter 12

NAME _____ DATE _____

Practice with Examples

For use with pages 745–750

EXAMPLE 2 *Applying the Distance Formula*

From your home, you ride your bicycle 5 miles north, then 12 miles east. How far are you from your home?

SOLUTION

You can superimpose a coordinate plane on a diagram of your bicycle trip. You start at the point $(0, 0)$ and finish at the point $(12, 5)$. Use the distance formula.

$$d = \sqrt{(12 - 0)^2 + (5 - 0)^2}$$
$$= \sqrt{144 + 25}$$
$$= \sqrt{169}$$
$$= 13$$

You are 13 miles from your home.

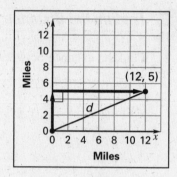

Exercise for Example 2

4. Rework Example 2 if you ride 8 miles east and 15 miles south.

EXAMPLE 3 *Finding the Midpoint Between Two Points*

Find the midpoint between $(-8, -4)$ and $(2, 0)$.

SOLUTION

Use the midpoint formula for the points (x_1, y_1) and (x_2, y_2): $\left(\dfrac{x_1 + x_2}{2}, \dfrac{y_1 + y_2}{2}\right)$.

$$\left(\frac{-8 + 2}{2}, \frac{-4 + 0}{2}\right) = \left(\frac{-6}{2}, \frac{-4}{2}\right) = (-3, -2)$$

The midpoint is $(-3, -2)$.

Algebra 1
Practice Workbook with Examples

NAME _____ DATE _____

Practice with Examples

For use with pages 745–750

Exercises for Example 3

Find the midpoint between the two points.

5. $(1, 3), (4, 5)$ **6.** $(6, 1), (-4, -1)$ **7.** $(6, 0), (0, 2)$

EXAMPLE 4 *Applying the Midpoint Formula*

You and a friend agree to meet halfway between your
two towns, as shown on the coordinate system at the right.
Find the location where you should meet.

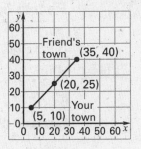

SOLUTION

The coordinates of your town are $(5, 10)$ and the
coordinates of your friend's town are $(35, 40)$. Use
the midpoint formula to find the point that is halfway
between the two towns.

$$\left(\frac{5 + 35}{2}, \frac{10 + 40}{2}\right) = \left(\frac{40}{2}, \frac{50}{2}\right)$$

$$= (20, 25)$$

You should meet at $(20, 25)$.

Exercise for Example 4

8. Rework Example 4 if the coordinates of your town are $(0, 35)$ and
the coordinates of your friend's town are $(30, 15)$.

Chapter 12

Practice with Examples

For use with pages 752–757

GOAL **Use the sine, cosine, and tangent of an angle and use trigonometric ratios in real-life problems**

VOCABULARY

A **trigonometric ratio** is a ratio of the lengths of two sides of a right triangle.

Sine, cosine, and **tangent** are the three basic trigonometric ratios. These ratios can be abbreviated as **sin, cos,** and **tan.**

EXAMPLE 1 *Finding Trigonometric Ratios*

For $\triangle ABC$, find the sine, the cosine, and the tangent of the angle.

a. $\angle A$

b. $\angle C$

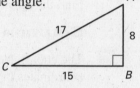

SOLUTION

a. For $\angle A$, the opposite side is 15 and the adjacent side is 8. The hypotenuse is 17.

$$\sin A = \frac{\text{opposite}}{\text{hypotenuse}} = \frac{15}{17}$$

$$\cos A = \frac{\text{adjacent}}{\text{hypotenuse}} = \frac{8}{17}$$

$$\tan A = \frac{\text{opposite}}{\text{adjacent}} = \frac{15}{8}$$

b. For $\angle C$, the opposite side is 8 and the adjacent side is 15. The hypotenuse is 17.

$$\sin C = \frac{\text{opposite}}{\text{hypotenuse}} = \frac{8}{17}$$

$$\cos C = \frac{\text{adjacent}}{\text{hypotenuse}} = \frac{15}{17}$$

$$\tan C = \frac{\text{opposite}}{\text{adjacent}} = \frac{8}{15}$$

Algebra 1
Practice Workbook with Examples

Chapter 12

NAME _____ DATE _____

Practice with Examples

For use with pages 752–757

Exercises for Example 1

Find the sine, the cosine, and the tangent of ∠A and ∠C.

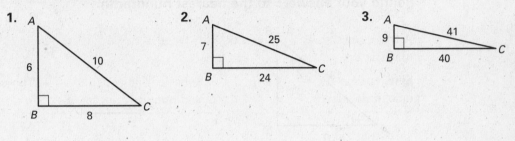

1.

2.

3.

EXAMPLE 2   *Solving a Right Triangle*

For $\triangle XYZ$, $z = 6$ and the measure of $\angle X$ is 60°. Find the length of y.

SOLUTION

You are given the side adjacent to $\angle X$, and you need to find the length of the hypotenuse.

$\cos X = \dfrac{\text{adjacent}}{\text{hypotenuse}}$ Definition of cosine

$\cos 60° = \dfrac{6}{y}$ Substitute 6 for z and 60° for $\angle X$.

$0.5 = \dfrac{6}{y}$ Use a calculator or a table.

$\dfrac{6}{0.5} = y$ Solve for y.

$12 = y$ Simplify.

The length y is 12 units.

NAME _____ DATE _____

Practice with Examples

For use with pages 752–757

Exercises for Example 2

Find the missing lengths of the sides of the triangle.
Round your answers to the nearest hundredth.

4.

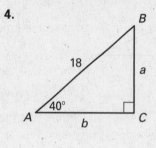

5.

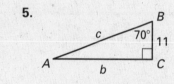

6.

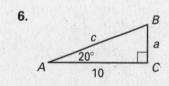

Algebra 1
Practice Workbook with Examples

NAME _____ DATE _____

Practice with Examples

For use with pages 758–764

GOAL Use logical reasoning and proof to prove that a statement is true and prove that a statement is false

---

VOCABULARY

Postulates or **axioms** are rules in mathematics that we accept to be true without proof.

Theorems are other new statements that have to be proved.

A **conjecture** is a statement that is believed to be true but not yet proved.

In an **indirect proof,** or a **proof by contradiction,** you assume that the original statement is false. If this leads to an impossibility, then the original statement is true.

EXAMPLE 1 *Proving a Theorem*

Prove the cancellation property of addition: If $a + c = b + c$, then $a = b$.

SOLUTION

$a + c = b + c$	Given
$a + c + (-c) = b + c + (-c)$	Addition axiom of equality
$a + [c + (-c)] = b + [c + (-c)]$	Associative axiom of addition
$a + 0 = b + 0$	Inverse axiom of addition
$a = b$	Identity axiom of addition

Exercises for Example 1

Prove the theorem using the basic axioms of algebra.

1. If $ac = bc$ and $c \neq 0$, then $a = b$.

2. If $a - c = b - c$, then $a = b$.

NAME _____ DATE _____

Practice with Examples

For use with pages 758–764

EXAMPLE 2 *Finding a Counterexample*

Assign values to a and b to show that the rule $\dfrac{1}{a + b} = \dfrac{1}{a} + \dfrac{1}{b}$ is false.

SOLUTION

You can choose any values of a and b, except $a = -b$, $a = 0$, or $b = 0$.
Let $a = 3$ and $b = 1$. Evaluate the left side of the equation.

$$\frac{1}{a + b} = \frac{1}{3 + 1} \qquad \text{Substitute 3 for } a \text{ and 1 for } b.$$

$$= \frac{1}{4} \qquad \text{Simplify.}$$

Evaluate the right side of the equation.

$$\frac{1}{a} + \frac{1}{b} = \frac{1}{3} + \frac{1}{1} \qquad \text{Substitute 3 for } a \text{ and 1 for } b.$$

$$= \frac{4}{3} \qquad \text{Simplify.}$$

Because $\dfrac{1}{4} \neq \dfrac{4}{3}$, you have shown one case in which the rule in false.

The counterexample of $a = 3$ and $b = 1$ is sufficient to prove that
$\dfrac{1}{a + b} = \dfrac{1}{a} + \dfrac{1}{b}$ is false.

Exercises for Example 2

**Find a counterexample to show that the statement is not
true.**

3. $\sqrt{a^2 + b^2} = a + b$

4. $a - b = b - a$

5. $a \div b = b \div a$

Algebra 1
Practice Workbook with Examples

NAME _____ DATE _____

Practice with Examples

EXAMPLE 3 *Using an Indirect Proof*

Use an indirect proof to prove the conclusion is true:

If $\dfrac{a}{b} \geq \dfrac{c}{b}$ and $b > 0$, then $a \geq c$.

SOLUTION

Assume that $a \geq c$ is not true. Then $a < c$.

$a < c$	Assume the opposite of $a \geq c$ is true.
$\dfrac{a}{b} < \dfrac{c}{b}$	Dividing each side by the same positive number produces an equivalent inequality.

This contradicts the given statement that $\dfrac{a}{b} \geq \dfrac{c}{b}$. Therefore, it is impossible that $a < c$.

You conclude that $a \geq c$ is true.

Exercise for Example 3

6. Use an indirect proof to prove that the conclusion is true:
   If $a + b > b + c$, then $a > c$.